D0328292

PRAYERS to the
GOD of my LIFE

Psalms for Morning and Evening

Early in the morning I cry out to you,
for in your word is my trust.
My eyes are open in the night watches,
that I may meditate upon your promise.

—Psalm 119:147–148

PRAYERS to the
GOD of my LIFE

Psalms for Morning and Evening

Lisa Belcher Hamilton

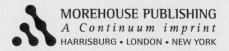

MOREHOUSE PUBLISHING
A Continuum imprint
HARRISBURG • LONDON • NEW YORK

Copyright ©2003 by Lisa Belcher Hamilton

Morehouse Publishing
P.O. Box 1321
Harrisburg, PA 17105

Morehouse Publishing is a Continuum imprint.

All rights reserved. No part of this book may be reproduced or transmitted in any form or by any means, electronic or mechanical, including photo-copying, recording, or by any information storage and retrieval system, without written permission from the publisher.

The psalms contained herein are from The Psalter in The Book of Common Prayer copyright © 1979 by The Church Hymnal Corporation, New York. Other Scripture quotations contained in the text are from the New Revised Standard Version Bible, copyright © 1989 by the Division of Christian Education of the National Council of Churches of Christ in the U.S.A. Used by permission. All rights reserved.

Design by Wesley Hoke

Library of Congress Cataloging-in-Publication Data

Hamilton, Lisa Belcher, 1959-
 Prayers to the God of my life : Psalms for morning and evening / Lisa Belcher Hamilton.
     p. cm.
Includes bibliographical references.
 ISBN 0-8192-1922-3 (pbk.)
 1. Bible. O.T. Psalms—Devotional use. 2. Bible. O.T. Psalms—Liturgical use. I. Title.
 BS1430.54 .H36 2003
 242'.8—dc21

2002153993

Printed in the United States of America
03 04 05 06 07   6 5 4 3 2 1

For Ted

That the generations to come might know,
and the children yet unborn;
that they in their turn might tell it to their children;
So that they might put their trust in God,
and not forget the deeds of God,
but keep God's commandments.

—Psalm 78:6–7

CONTENTS

Acknowledgements ix

Introduction xi

January 1

February 19

March 35

April 51

May 65

June 81

July 97

August 115

September 131

October 147

November 165

December 181

Recommended Resources 199

ACKNOWLEDGEMENTS

*T*his book has come to birth via some extraordinary midwives, and I wish to thank them all, especially the Sisters of St. Margaret for their example of living lives punctuated by and saturated with scripture; Phyllis Tickle for her encouragement of all who share her passion for religious writing; Cynthia Chapman Canaday for her enthusiastic friendship; Debra Farrington and the good folk at Morehouse for their editorial expertise; and my son, Ted, for his exuberant belief in his mother and endless tolerance of her time at the computer.

INTRODUCTION

*A*ll Christians employ themselves in David's Psalms more frequently than in any other part of the Old or New Testament. The grace of the Holy Ghost hath so ordered it that they should be sung every night and day. . . . Many who know not a letter can say David's Psalms by heart . . . where men converse with God, David is the first, the midst, and the last.

—*St. John Chrysostom (347–407)*

"Take two psalms and call me in the morning." Although she is an eminent professor of the Hebrew scriptures, it wasn't unusual for Ellen Davis to punctuate her lectures with humor, and this time I took her point to heart. A year into widowhood, I had moved my three-year-old and myself to New Haven, Connecticut to attend Yale Divinity School. I had no intention of seeking ordination; I was simply responding to my need to duke it out with God, who had allowed my husband to suffer and die of cancer at the age of thirty-two. Three mornings a week, I settled my son into preschool and wept and ranted through a therapy session before staggering into Professor Davis's class, frequently tardy, and nearly always feeling as though I'd put in a whole day already.

My fatigue was exacerbated because I had a hard time sleeping. Reading a few verses from the psalms at night gave my days a closure, and so I came to think of the psalms as healthy sleeping pills. Yet "sleeping pill" is a misnomer, because psalms are seldom lullabies. The psalms helped me sleep because I found in them every possible shade of human emotion—from self-pity to compassion—every possible hue of which I seemed to feel all at once, all the time.

The psalms became my permission slip to feel anything and everything I was feeling. Permission to live beyond the boxes of what I heard knowingly called "the grief process" by those who had yet to grieve. Permission to live in the knowledge that it was precisely my rage and loneliness and depth and range of pain that was maturing me. Permission to hear God whispering that loss fully felt bears gifts of wisdom and courage and freedom.

My story of the healing power of the psalms is only a stitch in the tapestry of meaning they have woven for countless human beings over thousands of years. Psalm by psalm, each frequently reworked, the Psalter (psalm book) was formed over hundreds of years on either side of the Babylonian exile in the late fifth century BCE. It can be agreed only that the development of what is known as the Psalter was long and complex and that some psalms were composed earlier in Israel's history than others.

In the first century CE, a convocation of rabbis meeting to determine what constitutes the Hebrew Bible included the psalms in the *Ketuvim* (writings) section, indicating their belief that the psalms are divinely inspired. The Psalter was included in the Christian Bible from the beginning, though Roman Catholics combine Psalms 10 and 11, which Protestants separate. Both traditions end up with a psalter of 150 psalms, although the numbering is off by one until Psalm 147. Numbering is but one wrinkle in the complicated history of the psalms, whose reconstruction calls for determining how a fluid expression of human relationship with God is modified and transmitted over the changes of situation and time. It is rather like figuring out which plants were used for the dye from which tapestry threads were colored. To further complicate the tapestry, a variety of pictures in the work have been modified by several artisans as the use of several psalms seems to have morphed over time, changing for instance from a personal poem to one that was incorporated into a liturgy used in corporate worship.

Most psalms seem to have begun as songs—indeed, the Hebrew title of the book, *Tehillim*, translates into English as "hymns," and the word "psalm" means "a striking of musical strings" in Greek. The rhythm of psalms served the practical purpose of aiding memory so they could be easily passed from generation to generation. Somewhat like educational folk songs, the psalms were teaching tools used by elders to transmit the history and culture of a developing Israel to its youngsters, as in Psalm 105:37–38: "Then he brought Israel out with silver and gold, and there was no one among their tribes who stumbled. Egypt was glad when they departed, for dread of them had fallen upon it."

Although early Christians insisted that King David (who died around 970 BCE) composed the psalms, current scholarship claims that it is more likely that the psalms marked with David's name are instead associated with, rather than authored by him, and that "of David" gives us no better clue to authorship than do the comments on musical instruments and notes to those who directed the worship in the temple.

Over the centuries, several ways of analyzing the psalms have evolved. Many have viewed the Psalter as a library holding five collections of psalms, each of which (except the last) ends with a doxology. Thus, some have concluded that these five collections (Psalms 1–41, Psalms 42–72, Psalms 73–89, Psalms 90–106, Psalms 107–150) had their beginnings in five separate communities of faith. Others have argued that the divisions may have little to do with their origin, and that the Psalter was divided arbitrarily into five books to reflect the five books that comprise the "Books of Moses," also called the Torah, or Pentateuch (Genesis, Exodus, Leviticus, Numbers, and Deuteronomy).

In the twentieth century, German scholars developed "form criticism" to analyze first the psalms and later the entire Bible. For example, the psalms can be divided into community psalms of lament ("O LORD God of hosts, how long will you be angered despite the prayers of your people? You have fed them with the bread of tears; you have given them bowls of tears to drink"—Psalm 80:4–5); individual psalms of lament ("How long shall I have perplexity in my mind, and grief in my heart, day after day? how long shall my enemy triumph over me?"—Psalm 13:2); community psalms of praise ("We have escaped like a bird from the snare of the fowler; the snare is broken, and we have escaped"—Psalm 124:7); individual psalms of praise ("You have turned my wailing into dancing; you have put off my sack-cloth and clothed me with joy"—Psalm 30:12); and psalms that seek to describe God ("Who is like the LORD our God, who sits enthroned on high, but stoops to behold the heavens and the earth?" —Psalm 113:5). Other scholars have categorized psalms according to the forms of secular literature that existed in the Middle East during early Israelite history.

More recently, scholars have posited that the psalms (indeed, all of the Bible) are beyond form, that they are in fact literature that is "anti-literature."[1] Although the psalmists, like all wordsmiths, were certainly conscious of the ways in which they worked with language, their purpose transcends language, as it is written in Ecclesiastes 12:12a–13, "Of making many books there is no end, and much study is a weariness of the flesh. The end of the matter; all has been heard. Fear God and keep his commandments; for that is the whole duty of everyone." Only writers of the sacred dare to make books whose purpose is fearing God.

A hallmark of the Bible in general, and particularly of the Psalter, is that it is meant to be interactive. A cookbook is meant to be used, but it is mere instruction and cannot be considered literature in the way in which a work such as *The Grapes of Wrath* can be. Although fine novels and poems and short stories may contain some life lessons, they are not intended to be used in the way a cookbook is. The psalms, however, transcend the categories of instruction and literature.

Like the best children's toys, the psalms demand interaction. Unlike a wind-up gizmo that children passively watch, the psalms insist that we play with them, that we bring our anger and needs and awe to them. Much as children develop in healthy ways when they play with toys like blocks and puppets that engage the imagination and invite emotional expression, by meeting the psalms' challenge of interaction we find ourselves engaged with God and invited to spiritual growth. As David L. Miller claims, "We don't pray the psalms. They pray us. . . . I have no idea where [a psalm] will take me. I don't know what desires it will awaken, what anger or fear, hope or joy will bubble up, or what long forgotten faces and experiences will appear out of nowhere."[2]

Furthermore, it is precisely the unsettling quality of the psalms that often transforms a barrier to God into a bridge.[3] Psalms are frequently jarring in their ugly emotion and image. Who among us wants to admit to wishing for God to "crush the heads of his enemies, and the hairy scalp of those who go on still in their wickedness" as in Psalm 68:21? The psalms stubbornly resist "political correctness" and thus they are frequently distasteful to our image of God, as in Psalm 97:3–4: "A fire goes before him and burns up his enemies on every side. His lightnings light up the world; the earth sees it and is afraid." God is presented as vengeful as well as violent as in 110:5–7: "The LORD who is at your right hand will smite kings in the day of his wrath; he will rule over the nations. He will heap high the corpses. . . ."

The psalms also often disturb our image of ourselves, as in 92:10: "My eyes also gloat over my enemies, and my ears rejoice to hear the doom of the wicked who rise up against me." Furthermore, several psalms agitate our view of the relationship between God and ourselves, as in 68:22–23: "The Lord has said, 'I will bring them back from Bashan; I will bring them back from the depths of the sea; That your foot may be dipped in blood, the tongues of your dogs in the blood of your enemies.'"

We are comfortable with God seeing us through our challenges and rescuing us from our enemies, as in Psalm 18:17–20: "He reached down from on high and grasped me; he drew me out of great waters. He delivered me from my strong enemies and from those who hated me; for they were too mighty for me. They confronted me in the day of my disaster; but the LORD was my support. He brought me out into an open place; he rescued me because he delighted in me." This comforting image of God like a doting aunt cooing over the cradle is, nevertheless, kin to the more shocking imagery found in the Psalter. Virtually all the imagery of the psalms challenges any vestige of complacency, leading us into a broader and more honest view of God, the world, and ourselves.

The psalms draw us to them like an itch, eliciting our theological scratching precisely because the God they portray dares to shatter our categories for the divine. Because we label conscious connection with God "prayer," which (unfortunately) connotes polite conversation, the psalms also shatter our categories for permissible prayer in startling ways. Working on this book early one morning, as I read "Even my best friend, whom I trusted, who broke bread with me, has lifted up his heel and turned against me" (Psalm 41:9), the face of an Episcopal priest in my past who was a needy minister turned betrayer came to me with such detail that I found myself recalling the ways in which she had hurt me, ticking off the list as if I were a prosecutor sure to win my case. This exercise was draining, and it felt as if I were hitting a well-worn wall with her name on it. "Forgive," the directive came to me in a firm, compassionate voice as I read in verse 12, "In my integrity you hold me fast, and shall set me before your face forever." It is clear: the only way to look God in the face is to receive integrity, and the only way to integrity in this fractured relationship is to forgive. The wall gives way to something large and freeing each time I do so. It is as if the psalmist literally leads me to a place where I see more dimensions in the faces of myself, my betrayer, and our God.

Save when the subject is Israel's history, all the composers of the psalms employ a device that is surely a secret of the Psalter's longevity: specifics are avoided, yet generalities are described in striking detail, as in 22:14–15 ("I am poured out like water; all my bones are out of joint; my heart within my breast is melting wax. My mouth is dried out like a pot-sherd; my tongue sticks to the roof of my mouth; and you have laid me in the dust of the grave"). The specifics of our lives are found within the psalm's generalities: When we're cried out, we feel poured out like water. When we're physically harmed, our bones can be out of joint. When we're heartsick, we feel the emotional equivalent of melting wax. When our mouths are dry, we may be ill—dry mouth is a common symptom of chemotherapy. When we feel hopeless, it can seem that God has lain us in a dusty grave.

Nearly forty percent of the psalms are songs of misery: cries of complaint, grief, rage, loneliness, sorrow.[4] Yet we rarely experience such psalms as annoying whines. The dignity and honesty of the psalmists' language elevates even the ugliest human emotions to a level that deserves a hearing. The psalms offer a hammock that is wide enough for all the times, and all the feelings of our lives. As a desert father put it, the psalms display "all the emotional states known to humanity,"[5] and so they give us words when we are beyond words. There is virtually no emotion or situation that does not have a counterpart in a psalm. Somewhere in this range among anxiety and peace, lament and praise, there is rest in a more balanced, more complete view of ourselves, the world, and God.

The permission the psalms give us to feel whatever we're feeling extends to whenever we're feeling it. As Martin Shannon has written, "For the psalmist, the greater fault is not to doubt, but to forget."[6] My experience of a psalm surprising me with the memory of a painful relationship is not unusual; neither is the experience of being led by the same psalm toward healing.

September 11, 2001 insists that remembering is important, and nowhere was this clearer in the months following than at St. Paul's Chapel. Like the psalms, St. Paul's—"the little chapel that stood"—was a place that was safe for any feeling, any memory, and thus a place offering much comfort for rescue workers and family and friends of the dead.

A small eighteenth-century chapel where George Washington worshipped after taking the oath at nearby Federal Hall, St. Paul's is located one block from where the Twin Towers once stood. Yet the chapel suffered not so much as a shattered pane of glass on September 11th. Like the psalms, St. Paul's favored the poor, serving as a homeless shelter as well as a place of worship and peace in the bustle of Lower Manhattan. Some believe it was the homeless folk who saved St. Paul's. The night of September 10th, they had opened some windows to let in the cooling breeze and that depressurizing effect prevented the impact of the towers' falling from destroying the chapel. Someone else said it was as if God's hand wrapped around the chapel and said, "No." In any case, St. Paul's Chapel seemed to be a preview of heaven, as the psalms—"My soul clings to you; your right hand holds me fast" (63:8)—can also be. All needs were met. Tables were heaped with lip balm and gum and gloves and cough drops. The loft was packed to the ceiling with paper towels and blankets and long underwear. Hot meals came round the clock from a makeshift kitchen—biscuits and grits and bacon and eggs giving way to soup and lasagna giving way to fried chicken and meat loaf and even chocolate cake at midnight. Cots with fresh sheets. Massages in Washington's pew box. Podiatrists caring for battered feet. From some pews, dazed, worn-out police and other workers staring into space, bathing in the quiet. From other pews, soft voices, chuckles, choked sobs, and snores. It was a common sight to find a burly firefighter snoring on a stuffed bunny for a pillow. When the recovery effort at Ground Zero ended, the historic pews were scuffed with marks left by work boots. The scuffs will stay, a sacramental reminder of St. Paul's ministry to those who served at Ground Zero. Every available surface, from the backs of pews to the walls, was covered with letters and drawings: this one a giant flag made of preschoolers' handprints in Pittsburgh, this one a banner from relatives of those who were killed in the Oklahoma Federal Building, and, from Alabama, taped to a pillar, in crayon on construction paper, Psalm 36:7: "How priceless is your love, O God! your people take refuge under the shadow of your wings." The notes and artwork and banners came so quickly that every night a volunteer was assigned to take some down to make room for the new. But this verse from Psalm 36 remained until the recovery effort ended. No one could walk by that pillar without recognizing God's wings in the shape of hot coffee and hand-warmers and cold soda, in the persons of volunteers who had boarded a bus and lost a day's work to spend twelve hours in this sacred space, in the healing hands of folk from the Carolinas who came to massage feet. God's people all, doing God's work of love in the midst of evil and destruction. As do the psalms.

Jesus himself relied on the psalms. Indeed, the Psalter is often referred to as "Jesus' Prayerbook." Inside him must have been what Professor Davis refers to as an echo chamber, a familiarity with the psalms so long and deep that his life reverberated with the life of the Psalter. It was probably as natural for him to express himself in the language of psalms as it is for us to say "Great minds think alike" when two of us share the same idea simultaneously.

The psalms were probably part of Jesus' home life, and certainly part of his life as an observant Jew, all of whom made a pilgrimage three times each year during the festivals that defined the season and served as enormous reunions for a family of faith. It was during a Passover festival that a prepubescent Jesus stayed behind in the temple, and it was during Passover that he entered Jerusalem, instituted the Eucharist,[7] and was crucified. The liturgy of all three festivals was saturated with psalms, especially 113–118, the *Hallel*, which praises God for mercy toward Israel and its people. At Jesus' last Passover, the crowds that spread cloaks and branches in his path sang a portion of the *Hallel*[8] to him: "Blessed is the one who comes in the name of the Lord! Hosanna in the highest." Some scholars believe the *Hallel* was the hymn Jesus and his disciples sang after the Last Supper and before going to the Mount of Olives.[9] Many Christian denominations, including my own (Episcopal), incorporate a portion of Psalm 118 in the Eucharist.

The most poignant example of Jesus' relationship with the psalms comes when he hangs on the cross and finds, in the Psalter, words for a situation that is beyond words. In the gospels of both Mark (15:34) and Matthew (27:46), Jesus' last words are from Psalm 22:1: "My God, my God, why have you forsaken me?" In the gospel of Luke (23:46), Jesus' last words are from Psalm 31:5: "Into your hands I commend my spirit." The bystanders' mocking offer of vinegar[10] echoes Psalm 69:23: "They gave me gall to eat, and when I was thirsty, they gave me vinegar to drink." Both the derision of Jesus[11] and the humiliation he endured when the Roman soldiers gambled for his clothing[12] are envisaged in Psalm 22, the psalm most commonly associated with Jesus' crucifixion: "All who see me laugh me to scorn; they curl their lips and wag their heads" (22:7) and "They stare and gloat over me; they divide my garments among them; they cast lots for my clothing" (22:17).

In imitation of Jesus' relationship with the psalms, Christianity has persistently given the Psalter a place of importance. Paul advised the Corinthians to bring order and purpose to their worship by including psalms.[13] The author of the letter to the Colossians advised new Christians, "Let the word of Christ dwell in you richly; teach and admonish one another in all wisdom; and with gratitude in your hearts sing psalms, hymns, and spiritual songs to God."[14]

Two hundred or so years later, the desert mothers and fathers adopted the arduous spiritual discipline of memorizing the entire Psalter and then chanting all 150 psalms, every day. Fourth-century Christians were advised to use the psalms in private as well as public worship by luminaries such as the scholar Jerome and Bishop Ambrose. Augustine of Hippo delighted in finding Christ or the church prefigured in as many psalms as he could (almost all). The beautifully illuminated devotional Books of Hours that have survived Europe's Middle Ages usually include psalms, frequently those deemed most penitential.

Martin Luther was known to have a particular fondness for the psalms, and only the psalms were allowed to be sung during worship in John Calvin's Geneva. The first book of any kind printed in America was *The Bay Psalm Book*, imprinted in 1640 for use among the Puritans, who, though they strove to purify the Church of England, followed the dictate in the Book of Common Prayer (1540) that "the Psalter shalbe red through once every Moneth." For those Christians who follow the Benedictine Rule, drawn up circa 540, the liturgy includes the entire Psalter every week. For Sister Marjorie Raphael, who has recited the psalms daily since her days as a novice in the Society of Saint Margaret in 1946, "The psalms are forever new."[15]

I believe that you will come agree with Sister Marjorie Raphael when you begin and end your day by praying with the psalms, as it has been my experience that framing the day with prayer opens the day for God, whose grace is forever new. Musicologist turned Episcopal priest Cynthia Bourgeault puts it this way: use "of the psalms at regular intervals every day [works to] 'tether' the mind in a beneficial spiritual disposition."[16]

After a few lines from a psalm for morning and evening, I have added a question or a realization that the psalm brought me as I chose it for you. I hope you will find my additions useful launching pads into prayer that will help you meet the psalms' demand for interaction. I further hope that this book will help you feel part of a community of prayer, populated by all those of us who use the psalms to deepen our awareness of God and to live our lives in ways that are more attentive to God's desires. Perhaps you will find, as has one member of this community of prayer, that psalms are "the scrim and you can see the luminous on the other side."[17] Whatever you find, when you use the psalms to help you pray you are linked with a tradition that includes Jesus Christ, and so it is a tradition that will surely bring you closer to God.

Notes

1. See, for instance, Harold Fisch, *Poetry with a Purpose: Biblical Poetics and Interpretation* (Bloomington, IN: Indiana University Press, 1988), introduction, 1–7.
2. David L. Miller, "Psalms and Sighs," *The Lutheran* (December 1997): 13.
3. Ibid., 13–14.
4. Martin Shannon, "The Psalter: A School of Prayer," *Crosspoint* (Spring, 2001): 28.
5. Cynthia Bourgeault, *Singing the Psalms: Psalm Booklet* (Boulder, CO: Sounds True, 1997), 5.
6. Shannon, "The Psalter," 25.
7. In the synoptic gospels (Mark, Matthew, and Luke), the Last Supper (the first Eucharist) occurs during Passover.
8. Mark 11:9–10, Matthew 21:9, Luke 19:38.
9. Matthew 26:30.
10. Mark 15:36, Matthew 27:48, and John 19:29.
11. Mark 15:29–30, Matthew 27:39–40, Luke 23:35.
12. Mark 15:24, Matthew 27:35, Luke 23:34, John 19:24.
13. 1 Corinthians 14:26.
14. Colossians 3:16.
15. Sister Marjorie Raphael of the Society of Saint Margaret, in a letter to the author, January 18, 2002.
16. Bourgeault, *Singing the Psalms*, 3.
17. Phyllis Tickle, speaking at the Trinity Institute, a conference of the Parish of Trinity Church in the City of New York, April 5, 2002.

PRAYERS TO THE GOD OF MY LIFE

�֎

JANUARY

January 1 ✿ Hope

Morning 65:12–14

You crown the year with your goodness,
and your paths overflow with plenty.
May the fields of the wilderness be rich for grazing,
and the hills be clothed with joy.
May the meadows cover themselves with flocks,
and the valleys cloak themselves with grain;
let them shout for joy and sing.

How do you hope God will crown this year with goodness?

Evening 18:29–31

You, O LORD, are my lamp;
my God, you make my darkness bright.
With you I will break down an enclosure;
with the help of my God I will scale any wall.
As for God, his ways are perfect;
the words of the LORD are tried in the fire;
he is a shield to all who trust in him.

Recall a time when God illuminated your darkness.

January 2 ✿ Praise

Morning 5:1–4

Give ear to my words, O LORD;
consider my meditation.
Hearken to my cry for help, my King and my God,
for I make my prayer to you.
In the morning, LORD, you hear my voice;
early in the morning I make my appeal and watch for you.
For you are not a God who takes pleasure in wickedness,
and evil cannot dwell with you.

In what ways do you experience God differently at different times of the day?

Evening 79:13
For we are your people and the sheep of your pasture;
we will give you thanks for ever
and show forth your praise from age to age.

Recall someone you have known who lived as a person of God. What kind of example does that person offer you?

January 3 ❀ Strength

Morning 37:24–25
Our steps are directed by the LORD;
he strengthens those in whose way he delights.
If they stumble, they shall not fall headlong,
for the LORD holds them by the hand.

Today, notice how God is holding you by the hand. How is God directing your steps?

Evening 55:17–19a
But I will call upon God,
and the LORD will deliver me.
In the evening, in the morning, and at noonday,
I will complain and lament,
and he will hear my voice.
He will bring me safely back from the battle waged against me.

How is God at work in the battles being waged against you?

January 4 ❀ Trust

Morning 28:1–2
O LORD, I call to you;
my Rock, do not be deaf to my cry;
lest, if you do not hear me,
I become like those who go down to the Pit.
Hear the voice of my prayer when I cry out to you,
when I lift up my hands to your holy of holies.

Notice times today when you feel God hears you.

Evening 28:7–9
Blessed is the LORD!
for he has heard the voice of my prayer.

The L*ORD* *is my strength and my shield;*
my heart trusts in him, and I have been helped;
Therefore my heart dances for joy,
and in my song will I praise him.

Is there a connection between trust and joy?

January 5 ❀ Seeking

Morning 61:1–4
Hear my cry, O God,
and listen to my prayer.
I call upon you from the ends of the earth
with heaviness in my heart;
set me upon the rock that is higher than I.
For you have been my refuge,
a strong tower against the enemy.
I will dwell in your house for ever;
I will take refuge under the cover of your wings.

What images of God as a refuge resonate with you?

Evening 119:1–2
Happy are they whose way is blameless,
who walk in the law of the L*ORD!*
Happy are they who observe his decrees
and seek him with all their hearts!

How did you observe the Lord's decrees today?

January 6 ❀ The Epiphany

(See Matthew 2:1–12)

Morning 68:28–31
Send forth your strength, O God;
establish, O God, what you have wrought for us.
Kings shall bring gifts to you,
for your temple's sake at Jerusalem.
Rebuke the wild beast of the reeds,
and the peoples, a herd of wild bulls with its calves.
Trample down those who lust after silver;
scatter the peoples that delight in war.

What gifts do you offer God?

Evening 72:11–14
All kings shall bow down before him,
and all the nations do him service.
For he shall deliver the poor who cries out in distress,
and the oppressed who has no helper.
He shall have pity on the lowly and poor;
he shall preserve the lives of the needy.
He shall redeem their lives from oppression and violence,
and dear shall their blood be in his sight.

Pray for, and plan on how you can act of behalf of, someone who has no helper.

January 7 ❀ Confession

Morning 99:1–3
The LORD is King;
let the people tremble;
he is enthroned upon the cherubim;
let the earth shake.
The LORD is great in Zion;
he is high above all peoples.
Let them confess his Name, which is great and awesome;
he is the Holy One.

How do you experience the power of God?

Evening 62:8–9
In God is my safety and my honor;
God is my strong rock and my refuge.
Put your trust in him always, O people,
pour out your hearts before him, for God is our refuge.

When is it easiest to pour out your heart before God?

January 8 ❀ Thanksgiving

Morning 9:1–2
I will give thanks to you, O LORD, with my whole heart;
I will tell of all your marvelous works.
I will be glad and rejoice in you;
I will sing to your Name, O Most High.

Try thanking God for every blessing you notice today. How does gratitude affect your relationship with God?

Evening 147:7–12
Sing to the LORD with thanksgiving;
make music to our God upon the harp.
He covers the heavens with clouds
and prepares rain for the earth;
He makes grass to grow upon the mountains
and green plants to serve mankind.
He provides food for flocks and herds
and for the young ravens when they cry.
He is not impressed by the might of a horse;
he has no pleasure in the strength of a man;
But the LORD has pleasure in those who fear him,
in those who await his gracious favor.

Recall ways God has given you pleasure today, and recall ways you have given God pleasure today.

January 9 ❀ Wisdom

Morning 14:1–2
The fool has said in his heart, "There is no God."
All are corrupt and commit abominable acts;
there is none who does any good.
The LORD looks down from heaven upon us all,
to see if there is any who is wise,
if there is one who seeks after God.

Can you recall a time when you were foolish and gained the wisdom to change?

Evening 139:16–17
How deep I find your thoughts, O God!
how great is the sum of them!
If I were to count them, they would be more in number than the sand;
to count them all, my life span would need to be like yours.

What do you think God thinks about?

January 10 ❀ Presence

Morning 139:6–9
Where can I go then from your Spirit?
where can I flee from your presence?
If I climb up to heaven, you are there;
if I make the grave my bed, you are there also.
If I take the wings of the morning
and dwell in the uttermost parts of the sea,
Even there your hand will lead me
and your right hand hold me fast.

Recall a time when you were aware of God's presence only in retrospect. What tends to make you less aware of that presence?

Evening 42:10
The LORD grants his loving-kindness in the daytime;
in the night season his song is with me,
a prayer to the God of my life.

When have you known night seasons in your life?

January 11 ❀ Counsel

Morning 68:1–3
Let God arise, and let his enemies be scattered;
let those who hate him flee before him.
Let them vanish like smoke when the wind drives it away;
as the wax melts at the fire, so let the wicked perish at the presence of God.
But let the righteous be glad and rejoice before God;
let them also be merry and joyful.

What kind of wickedness do you pray for God to melt?

Evening 16:7–9
I will bless the LORD who gives me counsel;
my heart teaches me, night after night.
I have set the LORD always before me;
because he is at my right hand I shall not fall.
My heart, therefore, is glad, and my spirit rejoices;
my body also shall rest in hope.

What is the relationship between your heart, your spirit, and your body?

January 12 ❀ Time

Morning 37:14–16
The Lord laughs at the wicked,
because he sees that their day will come.
The wicked draw their sword and bend their bow
to strike down the poor and needy,
to slaughter those who are upright in their ways.
Their sword shall go through their own heart,
and their bow shall be broken.

Recall a time when you have seen wickedness come back through the heart of an evildoer.

Evening 90:1–2
Lord, you have been our refuge
from one generation to another.
Before the mountains were brought forth,
or the land and the earth were born,
from age to age you are God.

Who, in a previous generation, taught you about God?

January 13 ❀ Inheritance

Morning 119:33–34
Teach me, O LORD, the way of your statutes,
and I shall keep it to the end.
Give me understanding, and I shall keep your law;
I shall keep it with all my heart.

What makes it difficult for you to keep God's statutes?

Evening 73:21–25
When my mind became embittered,
I was sorely wounded in my heart.
I was stupid and had no understanding;
I was like a brute beast in your presence.
Yet I am always with you;
you hold me by my right hand.
You will guide me by your counsel,
and afterwards receive me with glory.
Whom have I in heaven but you?

and having you I desire nothing upon earth.
How has God healed bitterness in your life?

January 14 ✿ Shelter

Morning 46:5–6
There is a river whose streams make glad the city of God,
the holy habitation of the Most High.
God is in the midst of her;
she shall not be overthrown;
God shall help her at the break of day.

What do you imagine life is like in the city of God?

Evening 5:12–15
Because of their many transgressions cast them out,
for they have rebelled against you.
But all who take refuge in you will be glad;
they will sing out their joy for ever.
You will shelter them,
so that those who love your Name may exult in you.
For you, O LORD, will bless the righteous;
you will defend them with your favor as with a shield.

How do you feel about asking God to punish?

January 15 ✿ Calls

Morning 66:1–3
Be joyful in God, all you lands;
sing the glory of his Name;
sing the glory of his praise.
Say to God, "How awesome are your deeds!
because of your great strength your enemies cringe before you.
All the earth bows down before you,
sings to you, sings out your Name."

What is it that makes certain hymns and songs your favorites?

Evening 120:1–2
When I was in trouble, I called to the LORD;
I called to the LORD, and he answered me.
Deliver me, O LORD, from lying lips

and from the deceitful tongue.

From what deceit do you desire God to deliver you?

January 16 ❀ Promise

Morning 37:36–39
Wait upon the LORD and keep his way;
he will raise you up to possess the land,
and when the wicked are cut off, you will see it.
I have seen the wicked in their arrogance,
flourishing like a tree in full leaf.
I went by, and behold, they were not there;
I searched for them, but they could not be found.
Mark those who are honest;
observe the upright;
for there is a future for the peaceable.

Recall a time when you saw wickedness flourish . . . and wither.

Evening 112:4
Light shines in the darkness for the upright;
the righteous are merciful and full of compassion.

What do you notice about yourself when you are upright?

January 17 ❀ Assistance

Morning 71:8–9
Let my mouth be full of your praise
and your glory all the day long.
Do not cast me off in my old age;
forsake me not when my strength fails.

Pray for the elderly.

Evening 113:6–8
He takes up the weak out of the dust
and lifts up the poor from the ashes.
He sets them with the princes,
with the princes of his people.
He makes the woman of a childless house
to be a joyful mother of children.

Recall great gifts, even miracles, that God has given you.

January 18 ✤ Salvation

Morning 17:6–8
I call upon you, O God, for you will answer me;
incline your ear to me and hear my words.
Show me your marvelous loving-kindness,
O Savior of those who take refuge at your right hand
from those who rise up against them.
Keep me as the apple of your eye;
hide me under the shadow of your wings.

What loving-kindness do you need for today?

Evening 85:7–9
Show us your mercy, O LORD,
and grant us your salvation.
I will listen to what the LORD God is saying,
for he is speaking peace to his faithful people
and to those who turn their hearts to him.
Truly, his salvation is very near to those who fear him,
that his glory may dwell in our land.

How can you help bring God's glory to dwell in our land?

January 19 ✤ Waiting

Morning 10:1–4
Why do you stand so far off, O LORD,
and hide yourself in time of trouble?
The wicked arrogantly persecute the poor,
but they are trapped in the schemes they have devised.
The wicked boast of their heart's desire;
the covetous curse and revile the LORD.
The wicked are so proud that they care not for God;
their only thought is, "God does not matter."

When do you feel frustrated with God?

Evening 62:6–7
For God alone my soul in silence waits;
truly, my hope is in him.
He alone is my rock and my salvation,
my stronghold, so that I shall not be shaken.

When you put all your hope in God, how do you find God working in surprising ways?

January 20 ❀ Instruction

Morning 94:11–14
The LORD knows our human thoughts;
how like a puff of wind they are.
Happy are they whom you instruct, O LORD!
whom you teach out of your law;
To give them rest in evil days,
until a pit is dug for the wicked.
For the LORD will not abandon his people,
nor will he forsake his own.

Meditate on wisdom that endures.

Evening 16:1–2
Protect me, O God, for I take refuge in you;
I have said to the LORD, "You are my Lord,
my good above all other."
All my delight is upon the godly that are in the land,
upon those who are noble among the people.

Pray for those people in whom you delight.

January 21 ❀ Safety

Morning 27:7–8
For in the day of trouble he shall keep me safe in his shelter;
he shall hide me in the secrecy of his dwelling
and set me high upon a rock.
Even now he lifts up my head
above my enemies round about me.

Ask God to relieve your anxiety, and the anxiety of others as well.

Evening 84:1–2
How dear to me is your dwelling, O LORD of hosts!
My soul has a desire and longing for the courts of the LORD;
my heart and my flesh rejoice in the living God.
The sparrow has found her a house
and the swallow a nest where she may lay her young;

by the side of your altars, O LORD of hosts,
my King and my God.

Where do you find God dwelling?

January 22 ❀ Mighty Acts

Morning 150:1–2
Hallelujah!
Praise God in his holy temple;
praise him in the firmament of his power.
Praise him for his mighty acts;
praise him for his excellent greatness.

Begin your day praising God and notice if it affects your day.

Evening 74:15–16
Yours is the day, yours also the night;
you established the moon and the sun.
You fixed all the boundaries of the earth;
you made both summer and winter.

Why do you think God included so many opposites when creating the world?

January 23 ❀ Protection

Morning 6:6–9
I grow weary because of my groaning;
every night I drench my bed
and flood my couch with tears.
My eyes are wasted with grief
and worn away because of all my enemies.
Depart from me, all evildoers,
for the LORD has heard the sound of my weeping.
The LORD has heard my supplication;
the LORD accepts my prayer.

Pray for those—maybe even yourself—who face the day worn out from weeping through the night just passed.

Evening 63:7–8
For you have been my helper,
and under the shadow of your wings I will rejoice.

My soul clings to you;
your right hand holds me fast.

Do you experience God primarily as a helper? A protector? A companion?

January 24 ✾ Frailty

Morning 89:46–47
How long will you hide yourself, O LORD?
will you hide yourself for ever?
how long will your anger burn like fire?
Remember, LORD, how short life is,
how frail you have made all flesh.

Do you ever experience God as angry?

Evening 25:3–4
Show me your ways, O LORD,
and teach me your paths.
Lead me in your truth and teach me,
for you are the God of my salvation;
in you have I trusted all the day long.

What paths is God teaching you?

January 25 ✾ Judgment

Morning 7:11–12
God is my shield and defense;
he is the savior of the true in heart.
God is a righteous judge;
God sits in judgment every day.

How would you describe God's judgment?

Evening 30:4–6
Sing to the LORD, you servants of his;
give thanks for the remembrance of his holiness.
For his wrath endures but the twinkling of an eye,
his favor for a lifetime.
Weeping may spend the night,
but joy comes in the morning.

For what do you hope?

January 26 ❀ Discernment

Morning 119:37
Turn my eyes from watching what is worthless;
give me life in your ways.

How do you discern between that which is worthless and that which is of God?

Evening 8:4–10
When I consider your heavens, the work of your fingers,
the moon and the stars you have set in their courses,
What is man that you should be mindful of him?
the son of man that you should seek him out?
You have made him but little lower than the angels;
you adorn him with glory and honor;
You give him mastery over the works of your hands;
you put all things under his feet:
All sheep and oxen,
even the wild beasts of the field,
The birds of the air, the fish of the sea,
and whatsoever walks in the paths of the sea.
O Lord our Governor,
how exalted is your Name in all the world!

In what ways do you exercise your mastery over God's creation?

January 27 ❀ Burdens

Morning 68:19–20
Blessed be the Lord day by day,
the God of our salvation, who bears our burdens.
He is our God, the God of our salvation;
God is the Lord, by whom we escape death.

What burdens do you offer God this morning?

Evening 141:1–3
O Lord, I call to you; come to me quickly;
hear my voice when I cry to you.
Let my prayer be set forth in your sight as incense,
the lifting up of my hands as the evening sacrifice.
Set a watch before my mouth, O Lord,

and guard the door of my lips;
let not my heart incline to any evil thing.

Visualize your prayer as incense wafting toward God.

January 28 ❈ Fear

Morning 27:1
The LORD is my light and my salvation;
whom then shall I fear?
the LORD is the strength of my life;
of whom then shall I be afraid?

Whom do you fear?

Evening 47:1–4
Clap your hands, all you peoples;
shout to God with a cry of joy.
For the LORD Most High is to be feared;
he is the great King over all the earth.
He subdues the peoples under us,
and the nations under our feet.
He chooses our inheritance for us,
the pride of Jacob whom he loves.

What does it mean to you to "fear"—a more modern translation might be "respect"—God?

January 29 ❈ Redemption

Morning 77:14–15
You are the God who works wonders
and have declared your power among the peoples.
By your strength you have redeemed your people,
the children of Jacob and Joseph.

How do you experience yourself as one of God's people?

Evening 119:97–100
Oh, how I love your law!
all the day long it is in my mind.
Your commandment has made me wiser than my enemies,
and it is always with me.
I have more understanding than all my teachers,

for your decrees are my study.
I am wiser than the elders,
because I observe your commandments.

With what wisdom has God blessed you?

January 30 ❀ Awaken

Morning 108:1–2
My heart is firmly fixed, O God, my heart is fixed;
I will sing and make melody.
Wake up, my spirit;
awake, lute and harp;
I myself will waken the dawn.

How does it feel when your spirit is fully awake?

Evening 37:28–29
Turn from evil, and do good,
and dwell in the land for ever.
For the LORD loves justice;
he does not forsake his faithful ones.

Imagine a land brimming with justice and devoid of evil.

January 31 ❀ Sure-Footing

Morning 18:32–34
For who is God, but the LORD?
who is the Rock, except our God?
It is God who girds me about with strength
and makes my way secure.
He makes me sure-footed like a deer
and lets me stand firm on the heights.

Pray that God will grant you strength and dexterity and confidence this day.

Evening 73:26–29
Though my flesh and my heart should waste away,
God is the strength of my heart and my portion for ever.
Truly, those who forsake you will perish;
you destroy all who are unfaithful.

But it is good for me to be near God;
I have made the LORD God my refuge.

What is especially "good" at this time in your relationship with God?

FEBRUARY

February 1 ✳ Delight

Morning 1:2–3
Their delight is in the law of the LORD,
and they meditate on his law day and night.
They are like trees planted by streams of water,
bearing fruit in due season, with leaves that do not wither;
everything they do shall prosper.

Thank God for a person in your life who delights in God's law.

Evening 18:1–2
I love you, O LORD my strength,
O LORD my stronghold, my crag, and my haven.
My God, my rock in whom I put my trust,
my shield, the horn of my salvation, and my refuge;
you are worthy of praise.

Recall a way God has strengthened you today.

February 2 ✳ The Presentation of Our Lord Jesus Christ in the Temple
(See Luke 2:22–40)

Morning 27:5–6
One thing have I asked of the LORD;
one thing I seek;
that I may dwell in the house of the LORD all the days of my life;
To behold the fair beauty of the LORD
and to seek him in his temple.

What above all else do you seek of the Lord?

Evening 138:1–4
I will give thanks to you, O LORD, with my whole heart;
before the gods I will sing your praise.

I will bow down toward your holy temple
and praise your Name,
because of your love and faithfulness;
For you have glorified your Name
and your word above all things.
When I called, you answered me;
you increased my strength within me.

Is there a connection between gratitude and experiencing your strength?

February 3 ❀ Restoration

Morning 126:5–7
Restore our fortunes, O LORD,
like the watercourses of the Negev.
Those who sowed with tears
will reap with songs of joy.
Those who go out weeping, carrying the seed,
will come again with joy, shouldering their sheaves.

Notice what you sow and what you reap today.

Evening 77:3–6
I think of God, I am restless,
I ponder, and my spirit faints.
You will not let my eyelids close;
I am troubled and I cannot speak.
I consider the days of old;
I remember the years long past;
I commune with my heart in the night;
I ponder and search my mind.

How do you combine communing with God and pondering what is on your mind?

February 4 ❀ Protection

Morning 109:28–30
Let my accusers be clothed with disgrace
and wrap themselves in their shame as in a cloak.
I will give great thanks to the LORD with my mouth;
in the midst of the multitude will I praise him;
Because he stands at the right hand of the needy,

to save his life from those who would condemn him.

How do you see God's relationship with the needy? What is your own relationship with the needy?

Evening 19:9–11
The fear of the LORD is clean and endures for ever;
the judgments of the LORD are true and righteous altogether.
More to be desired are they than gold, more than much fine gold,
sweeter far than honey, than honey in the comb.
By them also is your servant enlightened,
and in keeping them there is great reward.

What does the psalmist mean by "the fear of the LORD is clean"?

February 5 ❀ Confidence

Morning 26:1–5
Give judgment for me, O LORD,
for I have lived with integrity;
I have trusted in the Lord and have not faltered.
Test me, O LORD, and try me;
examine my heart and my mind.
For your love is before my eyes;
I have walked faithfully with you.
I have not sat with the worthless,
nor do I consort with the deceitful.
I have hated the company of evildoers;
I will not sit down with the wicked.

Bring confidence to your relationship with God today!

Evening 9:15–18
The ungodly have fallen into the pit they dug,
and in the snare they set is their own foot caught.
The LORD is known by his acts of justice;
the wicked are trapped in the works of their own hands.
The wicked shall be given over to the grave,
and also all the peoples that forget God.
For the needy shall not always be forgotten,
and the hope of the poor shall not perish for ever.

How does neglecting the needy and the poor create traps for us?

February 6 ❧ Deliverance

Morning 46:7–8
The nations make much ado, and the kingdoms are shaken;
God has spoken, and the earth shall melt away.
The LORD of hosts is with us;
the God of Jacob is our stronghold.

What do you pray that God's word will melt away this day?

Evening 70:1–4
Be pleased, O God, to deliver me;
O LORD, make haste to help me.
Let those who seek my life be ashamed
and altogether dismayed;
let those who take pleasure in my misfortune
draw back and be disgraced.
Let those who say to me "Aha!" and gloat over me turn back,
because they are ashamed.
Let all who seek you rejoice and be glad in you;
let those who love your salvation say for ever,
"Great is the LORD!"

How do you experience God in relationship to vengeance?

February 7 ❧ Competition

Morning 89:8–11
Who is like you, LORD God of hosts?
O mighty LORD, your faithfulness is all around you.
You rule the raging of the sea
and still the surging of its waves.
You have crushed Rahab of the deep with a deadly wound;
you have scattered your enemies with your mighty arm.
Yours are the heavens; the earth also is yours;
you laid the foundations of the world and all that is in it.

Rahab is the name of an evil sea monster, of Satan in disguise. Think of a raging, dangerous place that God has made safe for you.

Evening 77:12–13
I will meditate on all your acts
and ponder your mighty deeds.

Your way, O God, is holy;
who is so great a god as our God?

How do some of the gods that compete with God in our time differ from God?

February 8 ❀ Unity

Morning 133 (entire psalm)
Oh, how good and pleasant it is,
when brethren live together in unity!
It is like fine oil upon the head
that runs down upon the beard,
Upon the beard of Aaron,
and runs down upon the collar of his robe.
It is like the dew of Hermon
that falls upon the hills of Zion.
For there the LORD *has ordained the blessing:*
life for evermore.

Give thanks for a community—a workplace, a neighborhood, a family, a church, a club—in which you have seen the effects of healthy unity.

Evening 43:5–6
Why are you so full of heaviness, O my soul?
and why are you so disquieted within me?
Put your trust in God;
for I will yet give thanks to him,
who is the help of my countenance, and my God.

In what ways is your soul disquieted this night?

February 9 ❀ Love

Morning 102:25–27
In the beginning, O LORD, *you laid the foundations of the earth,*
and the heavens are the work of your hands;
They shall perish, but you will endure;
they all shall wear out like a garment;
as clothing you will change them,
and they shall be changed;
But you are always the same,
and your years will never end.

How do you feel about God's changelessness in relationship to change in your life?

Evening 89:1–2
*Your love, O L*ORD*, for ever will I sing;*
from age to age my mouth will proclaim your faithfulness.
For I am persuaded that your love is established for ever;
you have set your faithfulness firmly in the heavens.

What do you believe most strongly about God?

February 10 ✵ Trust

Morning 25:1–2
*To you, O L*ORD*, I lift up my soul;*
my God, I put my trust in you;
let me not be humiliated,
nor let my enemies triumph over me.
Let none who look to you be put to shame;
let the treacherous be disappointed in their schemes.

As you put your trust in God this day, notice how it affects you—and others.

Evening 118:14–7
*The L*ORD *is my strength and my song,*
and he has become my salvation.
There is a sound of exultation and victory
in the tents of the righteous:
*"The right hand of the L*ORD *has triumphed!*
*the right hand of the L*ORD *is exalted!*
*the right hand of the L*ORD *has triumphed!"*
I shall not die, but live,
*and declare the works of the L*ORD*.*

How have you experienced God's triumph this day?

February 11 ✵ Envy

Morning 49:16–20
Do not be envious when some become rich,
or when the grandeur of their house increases;
For they will carry nothing away at their death,

nor will their grandeur follow them.
Though they thought highly of themselves while they lived,
and were praised for their success,
They shall join the company of their forebears,
who will never see the light again.
Those who are honored, but have no understanding,
are like the beasts that perish.

How do you cope with envy?

Evening 121:3–4
He will not let your foot be moved
and he who watches over you will not fall asleep.
Behold, he who keeps watch over Israel
shall neither slumber nor sleep.

Rest knowing that God is ever-watchful.

February 12 ❀ Receiving

Morning 119:142–144
Your justice is an everlasting justice
and your law is the truth.
Trouble and distress have come upon me,
yet your commandments are my delight.
The righteousness of your decrees is everlasting;
grant me understanding, that I may live.

Whenever you are confused or frustrated this day, pray for understanding.

Evening 31:23–24
Love the Lord, *all you who worship him;*
the Lord *protects the faithful,*
but repays to the full those who act haughtily.
Be strong and let your heart take courage,
all you who wait for the Lord.

Receive God's gift of courage.

February 13 ❀ Stamina

Morning 18:36–37
You have given me your shield of victory;

your right hand also sustains me;
your loving care makes me great.
You lengthen my stride beneath me,
and my ankles do not give way.

Whenever you feel your confidence flagging today, remember that God's right hand sustains you.

Evening 34:4–8
I sought the LORD, and he answered me
and delivered me out of all my terror.
Look upon him and be radiant,
and let not your faces be ashamed.
I called in my affliction and the LORD heard me
and saved me from all my troubles.
The angel of the LORD encompasses those who fear him,
and he will deliver them.
Taste and see that the LORD is good;
happy are they who trust in him!

In what ways does your relationship with God bring you happiness?

February 14 ❋ Splendor

Morning 93:1–3
The LORD is King;
he has put on splendid apparel;
the LORD has put on his apparel
and girded himself with strength.
He has made the whole world so sure
that it cannot be moved;
Ever since the world began, your throne has been established;
you are from everlasting.

Remind yourself throughout the day that God's love is everlasting.

Evening 16:10–11
For you will not abandon me to the grave,
nor let your holy one see the Pit.
You will show me the path of life;
in your presence there is fullness of joy,
and in your right hand are pleasures for evermore.

Meditate on the fullness of joy.

February 15 ❀ Mortality

Morning 90:10–12

The span of our life is seventy years,
perhaps in strength even eighty;
yet the sum of them is but labor and sorrow,
for they pass away quickly and we are gone.
Who regards the power of your wrath?
who rightly fears your indignation?
So teach us to number our days
that we may apply our hearts to wisdom.

How is awareness of your mortality making you wise?

Evening 63:5–6

My soul is content, as with marrow and fatness,
and my mouth praises you with joyful lips,
When I remember you upon my bed,
and meditate on you in the night watches.

Find the places in your soul that are content.

February 16 ❀ Paths

Morning 58:3–7

The wicked are perverse from the womb;
liars go astray from their birth.
They are as venomous as a serpent,
they are like the deaf adder which stops its ears,
Which does not heed the voice of the charmer,
no matter how skillful his charming.
O God, break their teeth in their mouths;
pull the fangs of the young lions, O LORD.
Let them vanish like water that runs off;
let them wither like trodden grass.

Offer the wicked to God today.

Evening 61:5

For you, O God, have heard my vows;
you have granted me the heritage of those who fear your Name.

Recall someone in your past whose legacy to you includes faith.

February 17 ✤ Hope

Morning 119:49–52
Remember your word to your servant,
because you have given me hope.
This is my comfort in my trouble,
that your promise gives me life.
The proud have derided me cruelly,
but I have not turned from your law.
When I remember your judgments of old,
O Lord, I take great comfort.

How do God's laws bring you life?

Evening 149:4–5
For the Lord takes pleasure in his people
and adorns the poor with victory.
Let the faithful rejoice in triumph;
let them be joyful on their beds.

Recall ways you have given the Lord pleasure this day.

February 18 ✤ Crying

Morning 141:8–10
But my eyes are turned to you, Lord God;
in you I take refuge;
do not strip me of my life.
Protect me from the snare which they have laid for me
and from the traps of the evildoers.
Let the wicked fall into their own nets,
while I myself escape.

Pray to be aware of God's protection today.

Evening 77:1–2
I will cry aloud to God;
I will cry aloud, and he will hear me.
In the day of my trouble I sought the Lord;
my hands were stretched out by night and did not tire;
I refused to be comforted.

Even when we refuse to be comforted, God hears us.

February 19 ✸ Mercy

Morning 101:1–2

I will sing of mercy and justice;
to you, O LORD, will I sing praises.
I will strive to follow a blameless course;
oh, when will you come to me?
I will walk with sincerity of heart within my house.

Seek sincerity of heart this day.

Evening 104:1–3

Bless the LORD, O my soul;
O LORD my God, how excellent is your greatness!
you are clothed with majesty and splendor.
You wrap yourself with light as with a cloak
and spread out the heavens like a curtain.
You lay the beams of your chambers in the waters above;
you make the clouds your chariot;
you ride on the wings of the wind.

As you look at God's creation today, imagine God's light.

February 20 ✸ Revelation

Morning 71:5–7

For you are my hope, O Lord GOD,
my confidence since I was young.
I have been sustained by you ever since I was born;
from my mother's womb you have been my strength;
my praise shall be always of you.
I have become a portent to many;
but you are my refuge and my strength.

What was your relationship with God like when you were a child?

Evening 50:1–2

The LORD, the God of gods, has spoken;
he has called the earth from the rising of the sun to its setting.
Out of Zion, perfect in its beauty,
God reveals himself in glory.

How did you hear God speaking to the earth today?

February 21 ❀ Linger

Morning 1:1
Happy are they who have not walked in the counsel of the wicked,
nor lingered in the way of sinners,
nor sat in the seats of the scornful!

Pray for discernment throughout today, and notice whether it affects your actions.

Evening 55:1–4
Hear my prayer, O God;
do not hide yourself from my petition.
Listen to me and answer me;
I have no peace, because of my cares.
I am shaken by the noise of the enemy
and by the pressure of the wicked;
For they have cast an evil spell upon me
and are set against me in fury.

Hand over the noise of this day to God.

February 22 ❀ Shadows

Morning 91:1–2
He who dwells in the shelter of the Most High,
abides under the shadow of the Almighty.
He shall say to the Lord,
"You are my refuge and my stronghold,
my God in whom I put my trust."

How do you experience the shadow of God?

Evening 146:8–9
The Lord loves the righteous;
the Lord cares for the stranger;
he sustains the orphan and widow,
but frustrates the way of the wicked.
The Lord shall reign for ever,
your God, O Zion, throughout all generations.
Hallelujah!

Resolve to cooperate with God this day in caring for the needy.

February 23 ❀ Lifting

Morning 25:1–2

To you, O LORD, I lift up my soul;
my God, I put my trust in you;
let me not be humiliated,
nor let my enemies triumph over me.
Let none who look to you be put to shame;
let the treacherous be disappointed in their schemes.

Is there a relationship between lifting up your soul to God and deepening your trust in God?

Evening 138:7–8

Though the LORD be high, he cares for the lowly;
he perceives the haughty from afar.
Though I walk in the midst of trouble, you keep me safe;
you stretch forth your hand against the fury of my enemies;
your right hand shall save me.

Meditate on the hand of God.

February 24 ❀ Wonders

Morning 96:3–4

Declare his glory among the nations
and his wonders among all peoples.
For great is the LORD and greatly to be praised;
he is more to be feared than all gods.

Resolve to declare God's glory in the way you live today.

Evening 3:5–7

I lie down and go to sleep;
I wake again, because the LORD sustains me.
I do not fear the multitudes of people
who set themselves against me all around.
Rise up, O LORD; set me free, O my God;
surely, you will strike all my enemies across the face,
you will break the teeth of the wicked.

Pray for your enemies.

February 25 ❀ Safe Places

Morning 131:3
But I still my soul and make it quiet,
like a child upon its mother's breast;
my soul is quieted within me.

Resolve to still your soul throughout the day, and notice any ways this changes your day.

Evening 119:53–56
I am filled with a burning rage,
because of the wicked who forsake your law.
Your statutes have been like songs to me
wherever I have lived as a stranger.
I remember your Name in the night, O LORD,
and dwell upon your law.
This is how it has been with me,
because I have kept your commandments.

God is always a safe place for anger.

February 26 ❀ No Fear

Morning 119:149–151
Hear my voice, O LORD, according to your loving-kindness;
according to your judgments, give me life.
They draw near who in malice persecute me;
they are very far from your law.
You, O LORD, are near at hand,
and all your commandments are true.

Julian of Norwich claimed that God is as close as our own breath.

Evening 23:4
Though I walk through the valley of the shadow of death,
I shall fear no evil;
for you are with me;
your rod and your staff, they comfort me.

What role have these words played in your life?

February 27 ❀ Seasons

Morning 66:4–6
Come now and see the works of God,
how wonderful he is in his doing toward all people.
He turned the sea into dry land,
so that they went through the water on foot,
and there we rejoiced in him.
In his might he rules for ever;
his eyes keep watch over the nations;
let no rebel rise up against him.

Notice how wonderful God's "doings" are today.

Evening 104:20–21
You appointed the moon to mark the seasons,
and the sun knows the time of its setting.
You make darkness that it may be night,
in which all the beasts of the forest prowl.

How does God govern the seasons of your heart?

February 28 ❀ Safety

Morning 57:1
Be merciful to me, O God, be merciful,
for I have taken refuge in you;
in the shadow of your wings will I take refuge
until this time of trouble has gone by.

Go to God for safety.

Evening 92:1–4
It is a good thing to give thanks to the LORD,
and to sing praises to your Name, O Most High;
To tell of your loving-kindness early in the morning
and of your faithfulness in the night season;
On the psaltery, and on the lyre,
and to the melody of the harp.
For you have made me glad by your acts, O LORD;
and I shout for joy because of the works of your hands.

Which of God's acts have given you joy today?

February 29 ❁ Timing

Morning 108:11–13
Have you not cast us off, O God?
you no longer go out, O God, with our armies.
Grant us your help against the enemy,
for vain is the help of man.
With God we will do valiant deeds,
and he shall tread our enemies under foot.

Invite God into every deed.

Evening 102:11–12
My days pass away like a shadow,
and I wither like the grass.
But you, O LORD, endure for ever,
and your Name from age to age.

On this "extra" day, meditate on God's relationship to time.

MARCH

March 1 ❊ Right Spirit

Morning 51:11–12

Create in me a clean heart, O God,
and renew a right spirit within me.
Cast me not away from your presence
and take not your holy Spirit from me.

Notice those around you who possess a "right spirit."

Evening 42:11–15

I will say to the God of my strength,
"Why have you forgotten me?
and why do I go so heavily while the enemy oppresses me?"
While my bones are being broken,
my enemies mock me to my face;
All day long they mock me
and say to me, "Where now is your God?"
Why are you so full of heaviness, O my soul?
and why are you so disquieted within me?
Put your trust in God;
for I will yet give thanks to him,
who is the help of my countenance, and my God.

Place the heaviness of your soul in God's hands.

March 2 ❊ Watching

Morning 86:1–3

Bow down your ear, O LORD, and answer me,
for I am poor and in misery.
Keep watch over my life, for I am faithful;
save your servant who puts his trust in you.
Be merciful to me, O LORD, for you are my God;
I call upon you all the day long.

What role does God's listening play in your life?

Evening 69:3–4
I have come into deep waters,
and the torrent washes over me.
I have grown weary with my crying;
my throat is inflamed;
my eyes have failed from looking for my God.

Meditate on the gift of tears.

March 3 ❀ Sojourning

Morning 119:145–146
I call with my whole heart;
answer me, O LORD, that I may keep your statutes.
I call to you;
oh, that you would save me!
I will keep your decrees.

What are you calling out to God?

Evening 39:13–15
Hear my prayer, O LORD,
and give ear to my cry;
hold not your peace at my tears.
For I am but a sojourner with you,
a wayfarer, as all my forebears were.
Turn your gaze from me, that I may be glad again,
before I go my way and am no more.

What does it mean to sojourn with God?

March 4 ❀ Wholeness

Morning 49:6–8
We can never ransom ourselves,
or deliver to God the price of our life;
For the ransom of our life is so great,
that we should never have enough to pay it,
In order to live for ever and ever,
and never see the grave.

Meditate on the gift of eternal life.

Evening 19:13–14
Above all, keep your servant from presumptuous sins;
let them not get dominion over me;
then shall I be whole and sound,
and innocent of a great offense.
Let the words of my mouth and the meditation of my heart be acceptable
in your sight,
O LORD, my strength and my redeemer.

Watch for ways to avoid the sin of presumption today.

March 5 ❀ Trust

Morning 60:3–5
You have made your people know hardship;
you have given us wine that makes us stagger.
You have set up a banner for those who fear you,
to be a refuge from the power of the bow.
Save us by your right hand and answer us,
that those who are dear to you may be delivered.

If God made a banner for you today, what would it say?

Evening 22:4–5
Our forefathers put their trust in you;
they trusted, and you delivered them.
They cried out to you and were delivered;
they trusted in you and were not put to shame.

Pray for one of your ancestors of faith.

March 6 ❀ Scorn

Morning 69:10–13
Zeal for your house has eaten me up;
the scorn of those who scorn you has fallen upon me.
I humbled myself with fasting,
but that was turned to my reproach.
I put on sack-cloth also,
and became a byword among them.
Those who sit at the gate murmur against me,
and the drunkards make songs about me.

What eats up your soul?

Evening 6:3–4
My spirit shakes with terror;
how long, O LORD, how long?
Turn, O LORD, and deliver me;
save me for your mercy's sake.

What is most frightening to your spirit?

March 7 ❁ Cleansing

Morning 51:2–5
Wash me through and through from my wickedness
and cleanse me from my sin.
For I know my transgressions,
and my sin is ever before me.
Against you only have I sinned
and done what is evil in your sight.
And so you are justified when you speak
and upright in your judgment.

Offer your sins to God today.

Evening 119:28–29
My soul melts away for sorrow;
strengthen me according to your word.
Take from me the way of lying;
let me find grace through your law.

How has God strengthened you today?

March 8 ❁ Restoration

Morning 80:4–7
O LORD God of hosts,
how long will you be angered
despite the prayers of your people?
You have fed them with the bread of tears;
you have given them bowls of tears to drink.
You have made us the derision of our neighbors,
and our enemies laugh us to scorn.
Restore us, O God of hosts;
show the light of your countenance, and we shall be saved.

Meditate on the light of God's countenance.

Evening 119:35–36
Make me go in the path of your commandments,
for that is my desire.
Incline my heart to your decrees
and not to unjust gain.

Where does the path of God's commandments lead?

March 9 ❀ Frailty

Morning 89:46–47
How long will you hide yourself, O LORD?
will you hide yourself for ever?
how long will your anger burn like fire?
Remember, LORD, how short life is,
how frail you have made all flesh.

Remember today the frailties of those around you.

Evening 103:15–18
Our days are like the grass;
we flourish like a flower of the field;
When the wind goes over it, it is gone,
and its place shall know it no more.
But the merciful goodness of the LORD endures for ever on those who fear him,
and his righteousness on children's children;
On those who keep his covenant
and remember his commandments and do them.

Give thanks for the good that endures.

March 10 ❀ Repentance

Morning 7:1–5
O LORD my God, I take refuge in you;
save and deliver me from all who pursue me;
Lest like a lion they tear me in pieces
and snatch me away with none to deliver me.
O LORD my God, if I have done these things:
if there is any wickedness in my hands,

If I have repaid my friend with evil,
or plundered him who without cause is my enemy;
Then let my enemy pursue and overtake me,
trample my life into the ground,
and lay my honor in the dust.

If this psalm brings to mind any evil you have committed, confess it to God, asking forgiveness of God and any friend you have harmed.

Evening 70:5–6
But as for me, I am poor and needy;
come to me speedily, O God.
You are my helper and my deliverer;
O LORD, do not tarry.

Fill in the blank: God is my helper, my deliverer, and my _____.

March 11 ❀ Brokenness

Morning 51:9–10
Make me hear of joy and gladness,
that the body you have broken may rejoice.
Hide your face from my sins
and blot out all my iniquities.

Listen for joy and gladness today.

Evening 71:17–18
O God, you have taught me since I was young,
and to this day I tell of your wonderful works.
And now that I am old and gray-headed, O God, do not forsake me,
till I make known your strength to this generation
and your power to all who are to come.

What about God do you most hope to pass on?

March 12 ❀ Rescue

Morning 31:15–17
"My times are in your hand;
rescue me from the hand of my enemies,
and from those who persecute me.
Make your face to shine upon your servant,
and in your loving-kindness save me."

LORD, *let me not be ashamed for having called upon you;*
rather, let the wicked be put to shame;
let them be silent in the grave.

Remember today that your time is in God's hand.

Evening 51:15–17
Deliver me from death, O God,
and my tongue shall sing of your righteousness,
O God of my salvation.
Open my lips, O Lord,
and my mouth shall proclaim your praise.
Had you desired it, I would have offered sacrifice,
but you take no delight in burnt-offerings.

What sacrifices have you offered God this day?

March 13 ❀ Clarity

Morning 40:12–14
You are the LORD;
do not withhold your compassion from me;
let your love and your faithfulness keep me safe for ever,
For innumerable troubles have crowded upon me;
my sins have overtaken me, and I cannot see;
they are more in number than the hairs of my head,
and my heart fails me.
Be pleased, O LORD, *to deliver me;*
O LORD, *make haste to help me.*

Pray for the clarity and courage to see your sins.

Evening 119:30–32
I have chosen the way of faithfulness;
I have set your judgments before me.
I hold fast to your decrees;
O LORD, *let me not be put to shame.*
I will run the way of your commandments,
for you have set my heart at liberty.

What does it mean to possess a "heart at liberty"?

March 14 ✾ Purity

Morning 15:1–4
LORD, who may dwell in your tabernacle?
who may abide upon your holy hill?
Whoever leads a blameless life and does what is right,
who speaks the truth from his heart.
There is no guile upon his tongue;
he does no evil to his friend;
he does not heap contempt upon his neighbor.
In his sight the wicked is rejected,
but he honors those who fear the LORD.

Let no guile be upon your tongue this day.

Evening 51:8
Purge me from my sin, and I shall be pure;
wash me, and I shall be clean indeed.

What does it mean to be cleansed by God?

March 15 ✾ Rescue

Morning 69:1–2
Save me, O God,
for the waters have risen up to my neck.
I am sinking in deep mire,
and there is no firm ground for my feet.

From what do you desire God to save you?

Evening 116:2–4
The cords of death entangled me;
the grip of the grave took hold of me;
I came to grief and sorrow.
Then I called upon the Name of the LORD:
"O LORD, I pray you, save my life."
Gracious is the LORD and righteous;
our God is full of compassion.

How have you experienced God's compassion today?

March 16 ❀ Vision

Morning 123:1–3

To you I lift up my eyes,
to you enthroned in the heavens.
As the eyes of servants look to the hand of their masters,
and the eyes of a maid to the hand of her mistress,
So our eyes look to the LORD our God,
until he show us his mercy.

How would you describe your eyes in relationship to God?

Evening 89:48–51

Who can live and not see death?
who can save himself from the power of the grave?
Where, Lord, are your loving-kindnesses of old,
which you promised David in your faithfulness?
Remember, Lord, how your servant is mocked,
how I carry in my bosom the taunts of many peoples,
The taunts your enemies have hurled, O LORD,
which they hurled at the heels of your anointed.

What do you want God to remember about you?

March 17 ❀ Renewal

Morning 103:1–5

Bless the LORD, O my soul,
and all that is within me, bless his holy Name.
Bless the LORD, O my soul,
and forget not all his benefits.
He forgives all your sins
and heals all your infirmities;
He redeems your life from the grave
and crowns you with mercy and loving-kindness;
He satisfies you with good things,
and your youth is renewed like an eagle's.

Remind yourself of the renewed energy that comes from God's forgiveness.

Evening 42:3

My tears have been my food day and night,

while all day long they say to me,
"Where now is your God?"

How would you answer those who ask you, "Where now is your God?"

March 18 ❀ Nourishment

Morning 33:18–19
Behold, the eye of the LORD is upon those who fear him,
on those who wait upon his love,
To pluck their lives from death,
and to feed them in time of famine.

Notice all the ways God feeds you today.

Evening 56:8–9
You have noted my lamentation;
put my tears into your bottle;
are they not recorded in your book?
Whenever I call upon you, my enemies will be put to flight;
this I know, for God is on my side.

What sadness of yours do you hope God knows best?

March 19 ❀ Pity

Morning 6:1–2
LORD, do not rebuke me in your anger;
do not punish me in your wrath.
Have pity on me, Lord, for I am weak;
heal me, LORD, for my bones are racked.

From what do you require God's healing?

Evening 89:30–33
"If his children forsake my law
and do not walk according to my judgments;
If they break my statutes
and do not keep my commandments;
I will punish their transgressions with a rod
and their iniquities with the lash;
But I will not take my love from him,
nor let my faithfulness prove false."

How have you known God's faithfulness this day?

March 20 ❀ Mercy

Morning 103:9–11
He will not always accuse us,
nor will he keep his anger for ever.
He has not dealt with us according to our sins,
nor rewarded us according to our wickedness.
For as the heavens are high above the earth,
so is his mercy great upon those who fear him.

What is the relationship between your sins and God's mercy?

Evening 25:15–17
Turn to me and have pity on me,
for I am left alone and in misery.
The sorrows of my heart have increased;
bring me out of my troubles.
Look upon my adversity and misery
and forgive me all my sin.

What misery comes from sin?

March 21 ❀ Wounds

Morning 51:6–7
Indeed, I have been wicked from my birth,
a sinner from my mother's womb.
For behold, you look for truth deep within me,
and will make me understand wisdom secretly.

Look for truth deep within yourself this day.

Evening 109:20–21
But you, O Lord my GOD,
oh, deal with me according to your Name;
for your tender mercy's sake, deliver me.
For I am poor and needy,
and my heart is wounded within me.

Offer your wounds to God.

March 22 ❀ Progeny

Morning 144:11–13
Rescue me from the hurtful sword
and deliver me from the hand of foreign peoples,
Whose mouths speak deceitfully
and whose right hand is raised in falsehood.
May our sons be like plants well nurtured from their youth,
and our daughters like sculptured corners of a palace.

What metaphor do you wish for the generations that follow you?

Evening 14:3–4, 53:3–4
Every one has proved faithless;
all alike have turned bad;
there is none who does good; no, not one.
Have they no knowledge, those evildoers
who eat up my people like bread
and do not call upon God?

Offer your discouragement to God.

March 23 ❀ Stronghold

Morning 37:40–42
Transgressors shall be destroyed, one and all;
the future of the wicked is cut off.
But the deliverance of the righteous comes from the LORD;
he is their stronghold in time of trouble.
The LORD will help them and rescue them;
he will rescue them from the wicked and deliver them,
because they seek refuge in him.

What memories does God as a stronghold evoke for you?

Evening 13:1–2
How long, O LORD?
will you forget me for ever?
how long will you hide your face from me?
How long shall I have perplexity in my mind,
and grief in my heart, day after day?
how long shall my enemy triumph over me?

Recall times today when you felt God's face was hidden.

March 24 ✤ Bountiful

Morning 51:13–14

Give me the joy of your saving help again
and sustain me with your bountiful Spirit.
I shall teach your ways to the wicked,
and sinners shall return to you.

Take advantage of teachable moments today.

Evening 109:22–25

I have faded away like a shadow when it lengthens;
I am shaken off like a locust.
My knees are weak through fasting,
and my flesh is wasted and gaunt.
I have become a reproach to them;
they see and shake their heads.
Help me, O LORD my God;
save me for your mercy's sake.

Pray about the times you have felt shaken off this day.

March 25 ✤ The Annunciation
(See Luke 1:26–38)

Morning 43:3–4

Send out your light and your truth, that they may lead me,
and bring me to your holy hill
and to your dwelling;
That I may go to the altar of God,
to the God of my joy and gladness;
and on the harp I will give thanks to you, O God my God.

Notice opportunities to follow God's light and truth today.

Evening 37:17–18

The little that the righteous has
is better than great riches of the wicked.
For the power of the wicked shall be broken,
but the Lord upholds the righteous.

How have you seen the power of the wicked broken today?

March 26 ❀ Sight

Morning 119:17–18
Deal bountifully with your servant,
that I may live and keep your word.
Open my eyes, that I may see
the wonders of your law.

Thank God for the times your eyes are open today.

Evening 101:3–4
I will set no worthless thing before my eyes;
I hate the doers of evil deeds;
they shall not remain with me.
A crooked heart shall be far from me;
I will not know evil.

What does it mean to have "a crooked heart"?

March 27 ❀ Compassion

Morning 69:14–18
But as for me, this is my prayer to you,
at the time you have set, O LORD:
"In your great mercy, O God,
answer me with your unfailing help.
Save me from the mire; do not let me sink;
let me be rescued from those who hate me
and out of the deep waters.
Let not the torrent of waters wash over me,
neither let the deep swallow me up;
do not let the Pit shut its mouth upon me.
Answer me, O LORD, for your love is kind;
in your great compassion, turn to me."

Pray for patience to wait for the time God has set.

Evening 51:1
Have mercy on me, O God, according to your loving-kindness;
in your great compassion blot out my offenses.

What offenses committed this day do you desire God to blot out?

March 28 ❀ Weakness

Morning 6:1–2
LORD, do not rebuke me in your anger;
do not punish me in your wrath.
Have pity on me, LORD, for I am weak;
heal me, LORD, for my bones are racked.

How do you desire for God to heal you?

Evening 51:2–5
Wash me through and through from my wickedness
and cleanse me from my sin.
For I know my transgressions,
and my sin is ever before me.
Against you only have I sinned
and done what is evil in your sight.
And so you are justified when you speak
and upright in your judgment.

How do your sins hurt God?

March 29 ❀ Health

Morning 60:1–2
O God, you have cast us off and broken us;
you have been angry;
oh, take us back to you again.
You have shaken the earth and split it open;
repair the cracks in it, for it totters.

How do you desire that God repairs you?

Evening 38:1–4
O LORD, do not rebuke me in your anger;
do not punish me in your wrath.
For your arrows have already pierced me,
and your hand presses hard upon me.
There is no health in my flesh,
because of your indignation;
there is no soundness in my body, because of my sin.
For my iniquities overwhelm me;

like a heavy burden they are too much for me to bear.
Notice the health of offering the burden of your sin to God.

March 30 ❀ Understanding

Morning 119:25–27
My soul cleaves to the dust;
give me life according to your word.
I have confessed my ways, and you answered me;
instruct me in your statutes.
Make me understand the way of your commandments,
that I may meditate on your marvelous works.

Pray that your soul may cleave to that which is life-giving, instead of to the dust of that which is not.

Evening 69:5–6
Those who hate me without a cause are more than the hairs of my head;
my lying foes who would destroy me are mighty.
Must I then give back what I never stole?
O God, you know my foolishness,
and my faults are not hidden from you.

What foolishness came from your faults this day?

March 31 ❀ Sacrifice

Morning 51:18
The sacrifice of God is a troubled spirit;
a broken and contrite heart, O God, you will not despise.

Offer to God all that troubles you, all that breaks your heart.

Evening 119:169–170
Let my cry come before you, O LORD;
give me understanding, according to your word.
Let my supplication come before you;
deliver me, according to your promise.

Pray for the understanding God desires for you.

APRIL
The Exodus Story as
Told by Psalms 105–107

April 1 ❀ Naming

Morning 105:1–2
Give thanks to the LORD and call upon his Name;
make known his deeds among the peoples.
Sing to him, sing praises to him,
and speak of all his marvelous works.
Speak of God's marvelous works today.

Evening 105:3–4
Glory in his holy Name;
let the hearts of those who seek the LORD rejoice.
Search for the LORD and his strength;
continually seek his face.
How have you searched for God today?

April 2 ❀ Heritage

Morning 105:5–6
Remember the marvels he has done,
his wonders and the judgments of his mouth,
O offspring of Abraham his servant,
O children of Jacob his chosen.
Remember your heritage as a child of God.

Evening 105:7–8
He is the LORD our God;
his judgments prevail in all the world.
He has always been mindful of his covenant,

the promise he made for a thousand generations
How have you experienced God's covenant today?

April 3 ❀ Inheritance

Morning 105:9–11
The covenant he made with Abraham,
the oath that he swore to Isaac,
Which he established as a statute for Jacob,
an everlasting covenant for Israel,
Saying, "To you will I give the land of Canaan
to be your allotted inheritance."
Notice God's gifts to you.

Evening 105:12–15
When they were few in number,
of little account, and sojourners in the land,
Wandering from nation to nation
and from one kingdom to another,
He let no one oppress them
and rebuked kings for their sake,
Saying, "Do not touch my anointed
and do my prophets no harm."
How has God kept you safe today?

April 4 ❀ Enslavement

Morning 105:16–17
Then he called for a famine in the land
and destroyed the supply of bread.
He sent a man before them,
Joseph, who was sold as a slave.
Recall times when you have felt enslaved.

Evening 105:18–19
They bruised his feet in fetters;
his neck they put in an iron collar.
Until his prediction came to pass,
the word of the LORD tested him.
Have you ever felt God was testing you?

April 5 ❀ Release

Morning 105:20
The king sent and released him;
the ruler of the peoples set him free.

Acknowledge the freedom in your life.

Evening 105:21–22
He set him as a master over his household,
as a ruler over all his possessions,
To instruct his princes according to his will
and to teach his elders wisdom.

In what ways does God entrust you?

April 6 ❀ Fruitful

Morning 105:23–25
Israel came into Egypt,
and Jacob became a sojourner in the land of Ham.
The LORD *made his people exceedingly fruitful;*
he made them stronger than their enemies;
Whose heart he turned, so that they hated his people,
and dealt unjustly with his servants.

Notice the ways God gives you strength this day, and the ways in which you are fruitful.

Evening 105:26–27
He sent Moses his servant,
and Aaron whom he had chosen.
They worked his signs among them,
and portents in the land of Ham.

What signs is God calling you to work?

April 7 ❀ Portents

Morning 105:28–29
He sent darkness, and it grew dark;
but the Egyptians rebelled against his words.
He turned their waters into blood

and caused their fish to die.
Be attentive to God's power today.

Evening 105:30–31
Their land was overrun by frogs,
in the very chambers of their kings.
He spoke, and there came swarms of insects
and gnats within all their borders.

What blessings and challenges and insights have swarmed into your life today?

April 8 ✿ Devastation

Morning 105:32–33
He gave them hailstones instead of rain,
and flames of fire throughout their land.
He blasted their vines and their fig trees
and shattered every tree in their country.

Pray for all you notice that is shattered.

Evening 105:34–35
He spoke, and the locust came,
and young locusts without number,
Which ate up all the green plants in their land
and devoured the fruit of their soil.

What have you seen devoured in your life?

April 9 ✿ Sure-Footing

Morning 105:36–37
He struck down the firstborn of their land,
the firstfruits of all their strength.
He led out his people with silver and gold;
in all their tribes there was not one that stumbled.

Bring a conviction to this day that God will not allow you to stumble.

Evening 105:38–39
Egypt was glad of their going,
because they were afraid of them.

He spread out a cloud for a covering
and a fire to give light in the night season.

With what clouds of protection does God cover you?

April 10 ❀ Satisfaction

Morning 105:40–41
They asked, and quails appeared,
and he satisfied them with bread from heaven.
He opened the rock, and water flowed,
so the river ran in the dry places.

Notice the rivers in the dry places of today.

Evening 105:42–43
For God remembered his holy word
and Abraham his servant.
So he led forth his people with gladness,
his chosen with shouts of joy.

Recall times when you have felt God rejoicing in your joy.

April 11 ❀ Statutes

Morning 105:44–45
He gave his people the lands of the nations,
and they took the fruit of others' toil,
That they might keep his statutes
and observe his laws.
Hallelujah!

Notice how you are blessed by the fruits of others' toil this day.

Evening 106:1–2
Hallelujah!
Give thanks to the LORD, *for he is good,*
for his mercy endures for ever.
Who can declare the mighty acts of the LORD
or show forth all his praise?

Go to sleep this evening thanking God.

April 12 ❀ Justice

Morning 106:3–4
Happy are those who act with justice
and always do what is right!
Remember me, O LORD, with the favor you have for your people,
and visit me with your saving help.

Bring justice to your actions this day.

Evening 106:5
That I may see the prosperity of your elect
and be glad with the gladness of your people,
that I may glory with your inheritance.

Meditate on "glory" as a verb.

April 13 ❀ Defiance

Morning 106:6–7
We have sinned as our forebears did;
we have done wrong and dealt wickedly.
In Egypt they did not consider your marvelous works,
nor remember the abundance of your love;
they defied the Most High at the Red Sea.

Notice the abundance in your life.

Evening 106:8–10
But he saved them for his Name's sake,
to make his power known.
He rebuked the Red Sea, and it dried up,
and he led them through the deep as through a desert.
He saved them from the hand of those who hated them
and redeemed them from the hand of the enemy.

How have you been saved by God today?

April 14 ❀ Cravings

Morning 106:11–12
The waters covered their oppressors;
not one of them was left.

Then they believed his words
and sang him songs of praise.

What helps you believe the word of God?

Evening 106:13-14
But they soon forgot his deeds
and did not wait for his counsel.
A craving seized them in the wilderness,
and they put God to the test in the desert.

What cravings have you experienced today?

April 15 ❁ Exchange

Morning 106:15–17
He gave them what they asked,
but sent leanness into their soul.
They envied Moses in the camp,
and Aaron, the holy one of the LORD.
The earth opened and swallowed Dathan
and covered the company of Abiram.

In what ways do you feel leanness in your soul?

Evening 106:18–20
Fire blazed up against their company,
and flames devoured the wicked.
Israel made a bull-calf at Horeb
and worshiped a molten image;
And so they exchanged their Glory
for the image of an ox that feeds on grass.

What is the "golden calf" that tempts you most?

April 16 ❁ Neglectful

Morning 106:21–22
They forgot God their Savior,
who had done great things in Egypt,
Wonderful deeds in the land of Ham,
and fearful things at the Red Sea.

Remember to look for God in all things today.

Evening 106:23–24

So he would have destroyed them,
had not Moses his chosen stood before him in the breach,
to turn away his wrath from consuming them.
They refused the pleasant land
and would not believe his promise.

Who has stood before God on your behalf?

April 17 ❀ Petulance

Morning 106:25–27

They grumbled in their tents
and would not listen to the voice of the LORD.
So he lifted his hand against them,
to overthrow them in the wilderness,
To cast out their seed among the nations,
and to scatter them throughout the lands.

Strive to hear God in your grumbling.

Evening 106:28–31

They joined themselves to Baal-Peor
and ate sacrifices offered to the dead.
They provoked him to anger with their actions,
and a plague broke out among them.
Then Phinehas stood up and interceded,
and the plague came to an end.
This was reckoned to him as righteousness
throughout all generations for ever.

Have you observed God's righteousness today?

April 18 ❀ Snares

Morning 106:32–33

Again they provoked his anger at the waters of Meribah,
so that he punished Moses because of them;
For they so embittered his spirit
that he spoke rash words with his lips.

Avoid rash words today.

Evening 106:34–36

They did not destroy the peoples
*as the L*ORD *had commanded them.*
They intermingled with the heathen
and learned their pagan ways,
So that they worshiped their idols,
which became a snare to them.

What are some of the snares in your spiritual life?

April 19 ❀ Forfeiture

Morning 106:37–38

They sacrificed their sons
and their daughters to evil spirits.
They shed innocent blood,
the blood of their sons and daughters,
which they offered to the idols of Canaan,
and the land was defiled with blood.

Make no senseless sacrifices in your life this day.

Evening 106:39–40

Thus they were polluted by their actions
and went whoring in their evil deeds.
*Therefore the wrath of the L*ORD *was kindled against his people*
and he abhorred his inheritance.

Do you believe that God abhors?

April 20 ❀ Humility

Morning 106:41–43

He gave them over to the hand of the heathen,
and those who hated them ruled over them.
Their enemies oppressed them,
and they were humbled under their hand.
Many a time did he deliver them,
but they rebelled through their own devices,
and were brought down in their iniquity.

Notice the ways God delivers the oppressed.

Evening 106:44–45
Nevertheless, he saw their distress,
when he heard their lamentation.
He remembered his covenant with them
and relented in accordance with his great mercy.

Remember that God hears lamentation.

April 21 ❋ Pity

Morning 106:46–47
He caused them to be pitied
by those who held them captive.
Save us, O LORD our God,
and gather us from among the nations,
that we may give thanks to your holy Name
and glory in your praise.

Do not withhold your pity this day.

Evening 106:48
Blessed be the LORD, the God of Israel,
from everlasting and to everlasting;
and let all the people say, "Amen!"
Hallelujah!

Meditate on the phrase "from everlasting to everlasting."

April 22 ❋ Deliverance

Morning 107:1–2
Give thanks to the LORD, for he is good,
and his mercy endures for ever.
Let all those whom the LORD has redeemed proclaim
that he redeemed them from the hand of the foe.

What does it mean to feel redeemed?

Evening 107:3–4
He gathered them out of the lands;
from the east and from the west,
from the north and from the south.
Some wandered in desert wastes;

they found no way to a city where they might dwell.
Remember that God wanders with you.

April 23 ❀ Hunger

Morning 107:5-6
They were hungry and thirsty;
their spirits languished within them.
Then they cried to the LORD in their trouble,
and he delivered them from their distress.

Take your hunger, your thirst, and your languishing spirit to God this day.

Evening 107:7–9
He put their feet on a straight path
to go to a city where they might dwell.
Let them give thanks to the Lord for his mercy
and the wonders he does for his children.
For he satisfies the thirsty
and fills the hungry with good things.

How has God satisfied you today?

April 24 ❀ Gloom

Morning 107:10–12
Some sat in darkness and deep gloom,
bound fast in misery and iron;
Because they rebelled against the words of God
and despised the counsel of the Most High.
So he humbled their spirits with hard labor;
they stumbled, and there was none to help.

How can you help release those who are bound fast in misery?

Evening 107:13–14
Then they cried to the LORD in their trouble,
and he delivered them from their distress.
He led them out of darkness and deep gloom
and broke their bonds asunder.

How does it make a difference in your life when you cry to the Lord in your trouble?

April 25 ❀ Marvels

Morning 107:15–16
*Let them give thanks to the L*ORD *for his mercy*
and the wonders he does for his children.
For he shatters the doors of bronze
and breaks in two the iron bars.

Notice God's wonders today.

Evening 107:17–19
Some were fools and took to rebellious ways;
they were afflicted because of their sins.
They abhorred all manner of food
and drew near to death's door.
*Then they cried to the L*ORD *in their trouble,*
and he delivered them from their distress.

Cry to the Lord to be delivered from foolish ways.

April 26 ❀ Healing

Morning 107:20–22
He sent forth his word and healed them
and saved them from the grave.
*Let them give thanks to the L*ORD *for his mercy*
and the wonders he does for his children.
Let them offer a sacrifice of thanksgiving
and tell of his acts with shouts of joy.

What does it mean to "offer a sacrifice of thanksgiving"?

Evening 107:23–24
Some went down to the sea in ships
and plied their trade in deep waters;
*They beheld the works of the L*ORD
and his wonders in the deep.

Behold the wonders of the Lord in the depth of your sleep.

April 27 ❀ Wobbly

Morning 107:25–27
Then he spoke, and a stormy wind arose,
which tossed high the waves of the sea.
They mounted up to the heavens and fell back to the depths;
their hearts melted because of their peril.
They reeled and staggered like drunkards
and were at their wits' end.

Resolve to turn to God when you are at your wit's end.

Evening 107:28–30
Then they cried to the LORD in their trouble,
and he delivered them from their distress.
He stilled the storm to a whisper
and quieted the waves of the sea.
Then were they glad because of the calm,
and he brought them to the harbor they were bound for.

How do you imagine the harbor for which you are bound?

April 28 ❀ Conversion

Morning 107:31–32
Let them give thanks to the LORD for his mercy
and the wonders he does for his children.
Let them exalt him in the congregation of the people
and praise him in the council of the elders.

Resolve to praise God through your actions today.

Evening 107:33–35
The LORD changed rivers into deserts,
and water-springs into thirsty ground,
A fruitful land into salt flats,
because of the wickedness of those who dwell there.
He changed deserts into pools of water
and dry land into water-springs.

Give thanks for the water in your life, even if it is the water of tears.

April 29 ❀ Home

Morning 107:36–37
He settled the hungry there,
and they founded a city to dwell in.
They sowed fields, and planted vineyards,
and brought in a fruitful harvest.

Notice areas of your life in which you are sowing and in which you are harvesting.

Evening 107:38–40
He blessed them, so that they increased greatly;
he did not let their herds decrease.
Yet when they were diminished and brought low,
through stress of adversity and sorrow,
(He pours contempt on princes
and makes them wander in trackless wastes.)

Offer your stress to God.

April 30 ❀ Reflection

Morning 107:41–42
He lifted up the poor out of misery
and multiplied their families like flocks of sheep.
The upright will see this and rejoice,
but all wickedness will shut its mouth.

Resolve to speak of the good.

Evening 107:43
Whoever is wise will ponder these things,
and consider well the mercies of the Lord.

How does pondering the mercies of God bring wisdom?

MAY

May 1 ❀ Protection

Morning 3:1–3
Lord, how many adversaries I have!
how many there are who rise up against me!
How many there are who say of me,
"There is no help for him in his God."
But you, O Lord, are a shield about me;
you are my glory, the one who lifts up my head."
Be aware of God's protection this day.

Evening 29:2–3
Ascribe to the Lord the glory due his Name;
worship the Lord in the beauty of holiness.
The voice of the Lord is upon the waters;
the God of glory thunders;
the Lord is upon the mighty waters.
When have you heard the voice of God today?

May 2 ❀ Salvation

Morning 35:1–3
Fight those who fight me, O Lord;
attack those who are attacking me.
Take up shield and armor
and rise up to help me.
Draw the sword and bar the way against those who pursue me;
say to my soul, "I am your salvation."
How do you hear God's salvation in your life?

Evening 62:1–2
For God alone my soul in silence waits;
from him comes my salvation.
He alone is my rock and my salvation,

my stronghold, so that I shall not be greatly shaken.
What role does silence play in your soul?

May 3 ❀ Mystery

Morning 64:7–10
The human mind and heart are a mystery;
but God will loose an arrow at them,
and suddenly they will be wounded.
He will make them trip over their tongues,
and all who see them will shake their heads.
Everyone will stand in awe and declare God's deeds;
they will recognize his works.
The righteous will rejoice in the Lord *and put their trust in him,*
and all who are true of heart will glory.
Notice those around you today who are true of heart.

Evening 143:1–2
Lord, *hear my prayer,*
and in your faithfulness heed my supplications;
answer me in your righteousness.
Enter not into judgment with your servant,
for in your sight shall no one living be justified.
For what do you ask God's forgiveness this night?

May 4 ❀ Wounds

Morning 90:14–15
Satisfy us by your loving-kindness in the morning;
so shall we rejoice and be glad all the days of our life.
Make us glad by the measure of the days that you afflicted us
and the years in which we suffered adversity.
Be thankful today for all that your suffering has taught you.

Evening 116:5–8
The Lord *watches over the innocent;*
I was brought very low, and he helped me.
Turn again to your rest, O my soul,
for the Lord *has treated you well.*

For you have rescued my life from death,
my eyes from tears, and my feet from stumbling.
I will walk in the presence of the LORD
in the land of the living.

How has your soul been treated today?

May 5 ❀ Listening

Morning 135:15–18
The idols of the heathen are silver and gold,
the work of human hands.
They have mouths, but they cannot speak;
eyes have they, but they cannot see.
They have ears, but they cannot hear;
neither is there any breath in their mouth.
Those who make them are like them,
and so are all who put their trust in them.

How do we become like that which we idolize?

Evening 18:6–7
I called upon the LORD *in my distress*
and cried out to my God for help.
He heard my voice from his heavenly dwelling;
my cry of anguish came to his ears.

Have you felt that God heard you today?

May 6 ❀ Earthly Existence

Morning 119:19–20
I am a stranger here on earth;
do not hide your commandments from me.
My soul is consumed at all times
with longing for your judgments.

In what ways do you feel like a stranger?

Evening 72:5–7
He shall live as long as the sun and moon endure,
from one generation to another.
He shall come down like rain upon the mown field,

like showers that water the earth.
In his time shall the righteous flourish;
there shall be abundance of peace till the moon shall be no more.

How do you feel about God's sense of time? Angry? Hopeful?

May 7 ❀ Presence

Morning 142:1–2
I cry to the LORD with my voice;
to the LORD I make loud supplication.
I pour out my complaint before him
and tell him all my trouble.

Take all your troubles to God today.

Evening 139:10–13
If I say, "Surely the darkness will cover me,
and the light around me turn to night,"
Darkness is not dark to you;
the night is as bright as the day;
darkness and light to you are both alike.
For you yourself created my inmost parts;
you knit me together in my mother's womb.
I will thank you because I am marvelously made;
your works are wonderful, and I know it well.

Which of God's wonderful works did you marvel at most today?

May 8 ❀ Cheer

Morning 98:5–7
Shout with joy to the LORD, all you lands;
lift up your voice, rejoice, and sing.
Sing to the LORD with the harp,
with the harp and the voice of song.
With trumpets and the sound of the horn
shout with joy before the King, the LORD.

Offer your joy to the Lord today.

Evening 94:18–19
As often as I said, "My foot has slipped,"
your love, O LORD, upheld me.

When many cares fill my mind,
your consolations cheer my soul.

Recall the Lord's consolations to you.

May 9 ❀ Justice

Morning 43:1–2
Give judgment for me, O God,
and defend my cause against an ungodly people;
deliver me from the deceitful and the wicked.
For you are the God of my strength;
why have you put me from you?
and why do I go so heavily while the enemy oppresses me?

In what ways does your soul feel heavy?

Evening 8:1–3
O LORD our Governor,
how exalted is your Name in all the world!
Out of the mouths of infants and children
your majesty is praised above the heavens.
You have set up a stronghold against your adversaries,
to quell the enemy and the avenger.

How does the Lord govern your life?

May 10 ❀ Upheaval

Morning 2:1–2
Why are the nations in an uproar?
Why do the peoples mutter empty threats?
Why do the kings of the earth rise up in revolt,
and the princes plot together,
against the LORD and against his Anointed?

Pray for peace.

Evening 90:3–6
You turn us back to the dust and say,
"Go back, O child of earth."
For a thousand years in your sight are like yesterday when it is past
and like a watch in the night.
You sweep us away like a dream;

we fade away suddenly like the grass.
In the morning it is green and flourishes;
in the evening it is dried up and withered.

What do you know about God's power over death?

May 11 ❁ Silence

Morning 109:1–2
Hold not your tongue, O God of my praise;
for the mouth of the wicked,
the mouth of the deceitful, is opened against me.
They speak to me with a lying tongue;
they encompass me with hateful words
and fight against me without a cause.

Recall times when you have experienced God as silent.

Evening 23:1–3
The LORD is my shepherd;
I shall not be in want.
He makes me lie down in green pastures
and leads me beside still waters.
He revives my soul
and guides me along right pathways for his Name's sake.

How has God revived your soul today?

May 12 ❁ Response

Morning 44:23–26
Awake, O Lord! why are you sleeping?
Arise! do not reject us for ever.
Why have you hidden your face
and forgotten our affliction and oppression?
We sink down into the dust;
our body cleaves to the ground.
Rise up, and help us,
and save us, for the sake of your steadfast love.

When have you felt forgotten by God?

Evening 62:13–14
God has spoken once, twice have I heard it,

that power belongs to God.
Steadfast love is yours, O Lord,
for you repay everyone according to his deeds.

Have you heard God today?

May 13 ❀ Boundaries

Morning 28:3
Do not snatch me away with the wicked or with the evildoers,
who speak peaceably with their neighbors,
while strife is in their hearts.

Separate yourself from hypocrites today.

Evening 55:5–9
My heart quakes within me,
and the terrors of death have fallen upon me.
Fear and trembling have come over me,
and horror overwhelms me.
And I said, "Oh, that I had wings like a dove!
I would fly away and be at rest.
I would flee to a far-off place
and make my lodging in the wilderness.
I would hasten to escape
from the stormy wind and tempest."

What kinds of lodgings bring you rest?

May 14 ❀ Indications

Morning 18:26–28
With the faithful you show yourself faithful, O God;
with the forthright you show yourself forthright.
With the pure you show yourself pure,
but with the crooked you are wily.
You will save a lowly people,
but you will humble the haughty eyes.

Live in ways today that you wish God to reflect back.

Evening 41:1–3
Happy are they who consider the poor and needy!
the LORD will deliver them in the time of trouble.

The LORD preserves them and keeps them alive,
so that they may be happy in the land;
he does not hand them over to the will of their enemies.
The LORD sustains them on their sickbed
and ministers to them in their illness.

Recall times today when you considered the poor and the needy.

May 15 ❀ Assurance

Morning 118:5–6
I called to the LORD in my distress;
the LORD answered by setting me free.
The LORD is at my side, therefore I will not fear;
what can anyone do to me?

Begin today with confidence.

Evening 80:14–17
Turn now, O God of hosts, look down from heaven;
behold and tend this vine;
preserve what your right hand has planted.
They burn it with fire like rubbish;
at the rebuke of your countenance let them perish.
Let your hand be upon the man of your right hand,
the son of man you have made so strong for yourself.
And so will we never turn away from you;
give us life, that we may call upon your Name.

Recall ways God has tended you today.

May 16 ❀ Flattery

Morning 5:8–11
Lead me, O LORD, in your righteousness,
because of those who lie in wait for me;
make your way straight before me.
For there is no truth in their mouth;
there is destruction in their heart;
Their throat is an open grave;
they flatter with their tongue.
Declare them guilty, O God;

let them fall, because of their schemes.

Ask God to help you avoid speaking flattery only with your tongue.

Evening 63:3–4
For your loving-kindness is better than life itself;
my lips shall give you praise.
So will I bless you as long as I live
and lift up my hands in your Name.

How have you flattered God today with your actions?

May 17 ❀ Gifts

Morning 21:4–7
He asked you for life, and you gave it to him:
length of days, for ever and ever.
His honor is great, because of your victory;
splendor and majesty have you bestowed upon him.
For you will give him everlasting felicity
and will make him glad with the joy of your presence.
For the king puts his trust in the LORD;
because of the loving-kindness of the Most High, he will not fall.

What is the best gift God will give you today?

Evening 39:9–10
Deliver me from all my transgressions
and do not make me the taunt of the fool.
I fell silent and did not open my mouth,
for surely it was you that did it.

How has God protected you today?

May 18 ❀ Prayer

Morning 109:3–4
Despite my love, they accuse me;
but as for me, I pray for them.
They repay evil for good,
and hatred for my love.

Pray for those who hurt you.

Evening 60:10–12
Have you not cast us off, O God?
you no longer go out, O God, with our armies.
Grant us your help against the enemy,
for vain is the help of man.
With God we will do valiant deeds,
and he shall tread our enemies under foot.

What has given you confidence in God today?

May 19 ❁ Hands

Morning 95:4–7
In his hand are the caverns of the earth,
and the heights of the hills are his also.
The sea is his, for he made it,
and his hands have molded the dry land.
Come, let us bow down, and bend the knee,
and kneel before the LORD our Maker.
For he is our God,
and we are the people of his pasture and the sheep of his hand.
Oh, that today you would hearken to his voice!

What do you envision in God's hands this morning?

Evening 33:20–22
Our soul waits for the LORD;
he is our help and our shield.
Indeed, our heart rejoices in him,
for in his holy Name we put our trust.
Let your loving-kindness, O LORD, be upon us,
as we have put our trust in you.

How does it feel when you put your trust in God?

May 20 ❁ Endurance

Morning 9:19–20
Rise up, O LORD, let not the ungodly have the upper hand;
let them be judged before you.
Put fear upon them, O LORD;
let the ungodly know they are but mortal.

Pray for the ungodly.

Evening 136:5–9
Who by wisdom made the heavens,
for his mercy endures for ever;
Who spread out the earth upon the waters,
for his mercy endures for ever;
Who created great lights,
for his mercy endures for ever;
The sun to rule the day,
for his mercy endures for ever;
The moon and the stars to govern the night,
for his mercy endures for ever.

How has God shown you mercy today?

May 21 ❀ Pain

Morning 69:31–32
As for me, I am afflicted and in pain;
your help, O God, will lift me up on high.
I will praise the Name of God in song;
I will proclaim his greatness with thanksgiving.

Confront pain with praise this day.

Evening 18:17–20
He reached down from on high and grasped me;
he drew me out of great waters.
He delivered me from my strong enemies
and from those who hated me;
for they were too mighty for me.
They confronted me in the day of my disaster;
but the LORD was my support.
He brought me out into an open place;
he rescued me because he delighted in me.

How has God rescued you today?

May 22 ❀ Singing

Morning 138:5–6
All the kings of the earth will praise you, O LORD,
when they have heard the words of your mouth.
They will sing of the ways of the Lord,

that great is the glory of the L*ORD*.

How do you sing the ways of the Lord in your life?

Evening 142:3–5
When my spirit languishes within me, you know my path;
in the way wherein I walk they have hidden a trap for me.
I look to my right hand and find no one who knows me;
I have no place to flee to, and no one cares for me.
I cry out to you, O L*ORD*;
I say, "You are my refuge,
my portion in the land of the living."

How has God been your refuge today?

May 23 ✤ Isolation

Morning 38:11–12
My friends and companions draw back from my affliction;
my neighbors stand afar off.
Those who seek after my life lay snares for me;
those who strive to hurt me speak of my ruin
and plot treachery all the day long.

Where is God when you feel isolated?

Evening 101:6–8
My eyes are upon the faithful in the land, that they may dwell with me,
and only those who lead a blameless life shall be my servants.
Those who act deceitfully shall not dwell in my house,
and those who tell lies shall not continue in my sight.
I will soon destroy all the wicked in the land,
that I may root out all evildoers from the city of the L*ORD*.

How have you been God's servant today?

May 24 ✤ Envy

Morning 4:1–2
Answer me when I call, O God, defender of my cause;
you set me free when I am hard-pressed;
have mercy on me and hear my prayer.
"You mortals, how long will you dishonor my glory;
how long will you worship dumb idols

and run after false gods?"
Consider one of your false gods and resolve to avoid it this day.

Evening 73:1–3
Truly, God is good to Israel,
to those who are pure in heart.
But as for me, my feet had nearly slipped;
I had almost tripped and fallen;
Because I envied the proud
and saw the prosperity of the wicked.

What tripped you up today?

May 25 ✿ Height

Morning 84:5–6
Those who go through the desolate valley will find it a place of springs,
for the early rains have covered it with pools of water.
They will climb from height to height,
and the God of gods will reveal himself in Zion.

Look for the places of springs in this day.

Evening 1:4–6
It is not so with the wicked;
they are like chaff which the wind blows away.
Therefore the wicked shall not stand upright when judgment comes,
nor the sinner in the council of the righteous.
For the LORD knows the way of the righteous,
but the way of the wicked is doomed.

How have you seen wickedness doomed today?

May 26 ✿ Endurance

Morning 111:9–10
He sent redemption to his people;
he commanded his covenant for ever;
holy and awesome is his Name.
The fear of the LORD is the beginning of wisdom;
those who act accordingly have a good understanding;
his praise endures for ever.

Give thanks for a person in your life whose wisdom is grounded in fear (respect) of the Lord.

Evening 19:7–8
The law of the LORD is perfect and revives the soul;
the testimony of the LORD is sure and gives wisdom to the innocent.
The statutes of the LORD are just and rejoice the heart;
the commandment of the LORD is clear and gives light to the eyes.

Have you found gifts in God's law today?

May 27 ✤ Toward God

Morning 52:6–9
The righteous shall see and tremble,
and they shall laugh at him, saying,
"This is the one who did not take God for a refuge,
but trusted in great wealth
and relied upon wickedness."
But I am like a green olive tree in the house of God;
I trust in the mercy of God for ever and ever.
I will give you thanks for what you have done
and declare the goodness of your Name in the presence of the godly.

What will you be like in the house of God today?

Evening 143:5–6
I remember the time past;
I muse upon all your deeds;
I consider the works of your hands.
I spread out my hands to you;
my soul gasps to you like a thirsty land.

What is your soul like as you spread out your hands to God this night?

May 28 ✤ Voice

Morning 34:1–3
I will bless the LORD at all times;
his praise shall ever be in my mouth.
I will glory in the LORD;
let the humble hear and rejoice.
Proclaim with me the greatness of the LORD;

let us exalt his Name together.

Resolve to exalt God's name today.

Evening 59:7–9
They go to and fro in the evening;
they snarl like dogs and run about the city.
Behold, they boast with their mouths,
and taunts are on their lips;
"For who," they say, "will hear us?"
But you, O LORD, you laugh at them;
you laugh all the ungodly to scorn.

What makes God laugh?

May 29 ❀ Ownership

Morning 24:1–2
The earth is the LORD's and all that is in it,
the world and all who dwell therein.
For it is he who founded it upon the seas
and made it firm upon the rivers of the deep.

Do something to respect God's earth this day.

Evening 119:41–43
Let your loving-kindness come to me, O LORD,
and your salvation, according to your promise.
Then shall I have a word for those who taunt me,
because I trust in your words.
Do not take the word of truth out of my mouth,
for my hope is in your judgments.

How has trust in God affected your day?

May 30 ❀ Promises

Morning 64:1–4
Hear my voice, O God, when I complain;
protect my life from fear of the enemy.
Hide me from the conspiracy of the wicked,
from the mob of evildoers.
They sharpen their tongue like a sword,
and aim their bitter words like arrows,

That they may shoot down the blameless from ambush;
they shoot without warning and are not afraid.

Bring your complaints to God today.

Evening 119:147–148
Early in the morning I cry out to you,
for in your word is my trust.
My eyes are open in the night watches,
that I may meditate upon your promise.

Meditate on promises you believe God has made to you today.

May 31 ❀ The Visitation of the Blessed Virgin Mary

(See Luke 1:39–56)

Morning 68:24–26
They see your procession, O God,
your procession into the sanctuary, my God and my King.
The singers go before, musicians follow after,
in the midst of maidens playing upon the hand-drums.
Bless God in the congregation;
bless the LORD, you that are of the fountain of Israel.

What is your role in God's procession?

Evening 91:3–4
He shall deliver you from the snare of the hunter
and from the deadly pestilence.
He shall cover you with his pinions,
and you shall find refuge under his wings;
his faithfulness shall be a shield and buckler.

A buckler is often such a small shield that it can be worn on your arm; in what small ways has God shielded you today?

JUNE

June 1 ❀ Endurance

Morning 117 (entire psalm)
Praise the LORD, *all you nations;*
laud him, all you peoples.
For his loving-kindness toward us is great,
and the faithfulness of the LORD *endures for ever.*
Hallelujah!

Remind yourself of God's faithfulness in stressful moments today.

Evening 18:21–22
The LORD *rewarded me because of my righteous dealing;*
because my hands were clean he rewarded me;
For I have kept the ways of the LORD
and have not offended against my God.

How have you kept the ways of the Lord today?

June 2 ❀ Creation

Morning 136:1–5
Give thanks to the LORD, *for he is good,*
for his mercy endures for ever.
Give thanks to the God of gods,
for his mercy endures for ever.
Give thanks to the Lord of Lords,
for his mercy endures for ever.
Who only does great wonders,
for his mercy endures for ever.

Where do you notice mercy in God's creativity?

Evening 8:4–6
When I consider your heavens, the work of your fingers,
the moon and the stars you have set in their courses,
What is man that you should be mindful of him?

the son of man that you should seek him out?
You have made him but little lower than the angels;
you adorn him with glory and honor.

How has God been mindful of you today?

June 3 ✿ Learning

Morning 86:11
Teach me your way, O Lord,
and I will walk in your truth;
knit my heart to you that I may fear your Name.

Live today in the knowledge that your heart is knitted to God.

Evening 44:1–2
We have heard with our ears, O God,
our forefathers have told us,
the deeds you did in their days,
in the days of old.
How with your hand you drove the peoples out
and planted our forefathers in the land;
how you destroyed nations and made your people flourish.

What has God destroyed, and what has God made flourish in your life today?

June 4 ✿ Omnipresence

Morning 148:7–10
Praise the Lord from the earth,
you sea-monsters and all deeps;
Fire and hail, snow and fog,
tempestuous wind, doing his will;
Mountains and all hills,
fruit trees and all cedars;
Wild beasts and all cattle,
creeping things and winged birds.

Resolve to see God's creation praising God today.

Evening 29:10–11
The Lord sits enthroned above the flood;
the Lord, sits enthroned as King for evermore.

The LORD shall give strength to his people;
the LORD shall give his people the blessing of peace.

How has God given you strength today?

June 5 ✺ Prosperity

Morning 90:16–17
Show your servants your works
and your splendor to their children.
May the graciousness of the Lord our God be upon us;
prosper the work of our hands;
prosper our handiwork.

Ask God to prosper the work of your hands this day.

Evening 2:11–13
Submit to the LORD with fear,
and with trembling bow before him;
Lest he be angry and you perish;
for his wrath is quickly kindled.
Happy are they all
who take refuge in him!

How do you feel when you take refuge in God?

June 6 ✺ Marvels

Morning 104:10–12
You send the springs into the valleys;
they flow between the mountains.
All the beasts of the field drink their fill from them,
and the wild asses quench their thirst.
Beside them the birds of the air make their nests
and sing among the branches.

Notice how God quenches your thirsts today.

Evening 78:12–14
He worked marvels in the sight of their forefathers,
in the land of Egypt, in the field of Zoan.
He split open the sea and let them pass through;
he made the waters stand up like walls.
He led them with a cloud by day,

and all the night through with a glow of fire.

Recall the marvels God has worked for one of your spiritual ancestors (not necessarily kin).

June 7 ❀ Perception

Morning 100:1–2
Be joyful in the LORD, all you lands;
serve the LORD with gladness
and come before his presence with a song.
Know this: The LORD himself is God;
he himself has made us, and we are his;
we are his people and the sheep of his pasture.

What song does your soul sing to God this morning?

Evening 91:5–7
You shall not be afraid of any terror by night,
nor of the arrow that flies by day;
Of the plague that stalks in the darkness,
nor of the sickness that lays waste at mid-day.
A thousand shall fall at your side
and ten thousand at your right hand,
but it shall not come near you.

Confront any terror this night with confidence that you are safe in God.

June 8 ❀ Longing

Morning 42:1–2
As the deer longs for the water-brooks,
so longs my soul for you, O God.
My soul is athirst for God, athirst for the living God;
when shall I come to appear before the presence of God?

What simile would you use to describe the longing of your soul for God?

Evening 31:21–22
Blessed be the LORD!
for he has shown me the wonders of his love in a besieged city.

Yet I said in my alarm,
"I have been cut off from the sight of your eyes."
Nevertheless, you heard the sound of my entreaty
when I cried out to you.

Today, did you have more of the sense that God heard you or that God did not see you?

June 9 ❀ Preservation

Morning 102:1–3
LORD, hear my prayer, and let my cry come before you;
hide not your face from me in the day of my trouble.
Incline your ear to me;
when I call, make haste to answer me,
For my days drift away like smoke,
and my bones are hot as burning coals.

Do not hesitate to call on God with urgency.

Evening 32:8
You are my hiding-place;
you preserve me from trouble;
you surround me with shouts of deliverance.

With what shouts has God surrounded you today?

June 10 ❀ Trust

Morning 34:20–22
He will keep safe all his bones;
not one of them shall be broken.
Evil shall slay the wicked,
and those who hate the righteous will be punished.
The LORD ransoms the life of his servants,
and none will be punished who trust in him.

Notice how God keeps your bones safe today.

Evening 80:8–13
You have brought a vine out of Egypt;
you cast out the nations and planted it.
You prepared the ground for it;
it took root and filled the land.

The mountains were covered by its shadow
and the towering cedar trees by its boughs.
You stretched out its tendrils to the Sea
and its branches to the River.
Why have you broken down its wall,
so that all who pass by pluck off its grapes?
The wild boar of the forest has ravaged it,
and the beasts of the field have grazed upon it.

Which of God's acts in your life today do you find most puzzling?

June 11 ❀ Stronghold

Morning 59:18–20
For my part, I will sing of your strength;
I will celebrate your love in the morning;
For you have become my stronghold,
a refuge in the day of my trouble.
To you, O my Strength, will I sing;
for you, O God, are my stronghold and my merciful God.

Find a concrete way to celebrate God's love today.

Evening 22:1–2
My God, my God, why have you forsaken me?
and are so far from my cry
and from the words of my distress?
O my God, I cry in the daytime, but you do not answer;
by night as well, but I find no rest.

What keeps you from rest?

June 12 ❀ Surety

Morning 93:1–3
The LORD is King;
he has put on splendid apparel;
the LORD has put on his apparel
and girded himself with strength.
He has made the whole world so sure
that it cannot be moved;
Ever since the world began, your throne has been established;

you are from everlasting.

What will you see today that is splendid enough to be God's clothing?

Evening 116:1
I love the LORD, *because he has heard the voice of my supplication,*
because he has inclined his ear to me whenever I called upon him.

Recall the times today when you knew God's ear was inclined toward you.

June 13 ❀ Judgments

Morning 35:4–5
Let those who seek after my life be shamed and humbled,
let those who plot my ruin fall back and be dismayed.
Let them be like chaff before the wind,
and let the angel of the LORD *drive them away.*

How does it feel to put your enemies in God's hands?

Evening 18:23–25
For all his judgments are before my eyes,
and his decrees I have not put away from me;
For I have been blameless with him
and have kept myself from iniquity;
Therefore the LORD *rewarded me according to my righteous dealing,*
because of the cleanness of my hands in his sight.

Do you think you were rewarded today for your actions?

June 14 ❀ Aging

Morning 119:9–10
How shall a young man cleanse his way?
By keeping to your words.
With my whole heart I seek you;
let me not stray from your commandments

Strive to cleanse your way today.

Evening 37:26–27
I have been young and now I am old,
but never have I seen the righteous forsaken,

or their children begging bread.
The righteous are always generous in their lending,
and·their children shall be a blessing.

How has your view of the world changed as you have aged?

June 15 ❀ Mystery

Morning 144:1–2
Blessed be the LORD my rock!
who trains my hands to fight and my fingers to battle;
My help and my fortress, my stronghold and my deliverer,
my shield in whom I trust,
who subdues the peoples under me.

Remember this day that God is present in all battles.

Evening 92:5–7
LORD, how great are your works!
your thoughts are very deep.
The dullard does not know,
nor does the fool understand,
that though the wicked grow like weeds,
and all the workers of iniquity flourish,
They flourish only to be destroyed for ever;
but you, O LORD, are exalted for evermore.

What have you been unable to understand about God today?

June 16 ❀ Safety

Morning 108:3–6
I will confess you among the peoples, O LORD;
I will sing praises to you among the nations.
For your loving-kindness is greater than the heavens,
and your faithfulness reaches to the clouds.
Exalt yourself above the heavens, O God,
and your glory over all the earth.
So that those who are dear to you may be delivered,
save with your right hand and answer me.

Pray for those who are dear to you, knowing that they are also dear
to God.

Evening 63:9–10
May those who seek my life to destroy it
go down into the depths of the earth;
Let them fall upon the edge of the sword,
and let them be food for jackals.

Any emotion is safe with God.

June 17 ❀ Power

Morning 110:1–3
The LORD said to my LORD, "Sit at my right hand,
until I make your enemies your footstool."
The LORD will send the scepter of your power out of Zion,
saying, "Rule over your enemies round about you.
Princely state has been yours from the day of your birth;
in the beauty of holiness have I begotten you,
like dew from the womb of the morning."

You are born to be in a holy state.

Evening 7:6–7
Stand up, O LORD, in your wrath;
rise up against the fury of my enemies.
Awake, O my God, decree justice;
let the assembly of the peoples gather round you.

Beckon God to battle on your behalf as you sleep.

June 18 ❀ Memory

Morning 53:5–6
See how greatly they tremble,
such trembling as never was;
for God has scattered the bones of the enemy;
they are put to shame, because God has rejected them.
Oh, that Israel's deliverance would come out of Zion!
when God restores the fortunes of his people
Jacob will rejoice and Israel be glad.

Pray for those in whom you see shame today.

Evening 136:23–26
[It is God] who remembered us in our low estate,

for his mercy endures for ever;
And delivered us from our enemies,
for his mercy endures for ever;
Who gives food to all creatures,
for his mercy endures for ever.
Give thanks to the God of heaven,
for his mercy endures for ever.

Remember that God's mercy extends to all creatures.

June 19 ❀ Companionship

Morning 99:4–5
"O mighty King, lover of justice,
you have established equity;
you have executed justice and righteousness in Jacob."
Proclaim the greatness of the LORD *our God*
and fall down before his footstool;
he is the Holy One.

Notice God's love of justice today.

Evening 88:17–19
Your blazing anger has swept over me;
your terrors have destroyed me;
They surround me all day long like a flood;
they encompass me on every side.
My friend and my neighbor you have put away from me,
and darkness is my only companion.

Even when you do not like God, God is your companion.

June 20 ❀ Creativity

Morning 138:9
The LORD *will make good his purpose for me;*
O LORD, *your love endures for ever;*
do not abandon the works of your hands.

Know that you are a work of God's hands.

Evening 19:1–4
The heavens declare the glory of God,

and the firmament shows his handiwork.
One day tells its tale to another,
and one night imparts knowledge to another.
Although they have no words or language,
and their voices are not heard,
Their sound has gone out into all lands,
and their message to the ends of the world.

What messages have *you* sent today?

June 21 ❀ Restoration

Morning 8:7–10
You give him mastery over the works of your hands;
you put all things under his feet:
All sheep and oxen,
even the wild beasts of the field,
The birds of the air, the fish of the sea,
and whatsoever walks in the paths of the sea.
O Lord our Governor,
how exalted is your Name in all the world!

Do something to help restore God's creation today.

Evening 30:1–3
I will exalt you, O LORD,
because you have lifted me up
and have not let my enemies triumph over me.
O Lord my God, I cried out to you,
and you restored me to health.
You brought me up, O LORD, from the dead;
you restored my life as I was going down to the grave.

How has God brought you up from "the dead" today?

June 22 ❀ Authority

Morning 68:21–23
God shall crush the heads of his enemies,
and the hairy scalp of those who go on still in their wickedness.
The LORD has said, "I will bring them back from Bashan;
I will bring them back from the depths of the sea;
That your foot may be dipped in blood,

the tongues of your dogs in the blood of your enemies."
No need for *you* to harm your enemies!

Evening 22:27–28
For kingship belongs to the LORD;
he rules over the nations.
To him alone all who sleep in the earth bow down in worship;
all who go down to the dust fall before him.
What do you think the worship life of the dead is like?

June 23 ❀ Praises

Morning 98:8–10
Let the sea make a noise and all that is in it,
the lands and those who dwell therein.
Let the rivers clap their hands,
and let the hills ring out with joy before the LORD,
when he comes to judge the earth.
In righteousness shall he judge the world
and the peoples with equity.
Listen for ways nature praises God.

Evening 119:21–24
You have rebuked the insolent;
cursed are they who stray from your commandments!
Turn from me shame and rebuke,
for I have kept your decrees.
Even though rulers sit and plot against me,
I will meditate on your statutes.
For your decrees are my delight,
and they are my counselors.
How do you delight in God's decrees?

June 24 ❀ Sound and Sight

Morning 29:1–3
Ascribe to the LORD, you gods,
ascribe to the LORD glory and strength.
Ascribe to the LORD the glory due his Name;
worship the LORD in the beauty of holiness.

The voice of the LORD is upon the waters;
the God of glory thunders;
the LORD is upon the mighty waters.

Listen for the sounds of God this day.

Evening 33:13–15
The LORD looks down from heaven,
and beholds all the people in the world.
From where he sits enthroned he turns his gaze
on all who dwell on the earth.
He fashions all the hearts of them
and understands all their works.

How do you think God understands the works you performed today?

June 25 ❀ The Wicked

Morning 3:7–8
Rise up, O LORD; set me free, O my God;
surely, you will strike all my enemies across the face,
you will break the teeth of the wicked.
Deliverance belongs to the LORD.
Your blessing be upon your people!

How do you feel about the image of the Lord breaking the teeth of the wicked?

Evening 89:22–24
No enemy shall deceive him,
nor any wicked man bring him down.
I will crush his foes before him
and strike down those who hate him.
My faithfulness and love shall be with him,
and he shall be victorious through my Name.

What helps you find God's faithfulness and love when you are under attack?

June 26 ❀ Listening

Morning 86:6–7
Give ear, O LORD, to my prayer,
and attend to the voice of my supplications.

In the time of my trouble I will call upon you,
for you will answer me.

Notice the ways you and others voice your supplications today, and call upon God with what you have noticed.

Evening 36:1–4
There is a voice of rebellion deep in the heart of the wicked;
there is no fear of God before his eyes.
He flatters himself in his own eyes
that his hateful sin will not be found out.
The words of his mouth are wicked and deceitful,
he has left off acting wisely and doing good.
He thinks up wickedness upon his bed
and has set himself in no good way;
he does not abhor that which is evil.

Think up honesty upon your bed this night.

June 27 ❁ Distance

Morning 120:3–5
What shall be done to you, and what more besides,
O you deceitful tongue?
The sharpened arrows of a warrior,
along with hot glowing coals.
How hateful it is that I must lodge in Meshech
and dwell among the tents of Kedar!

Is it better to be close to, or apart from, your enemies?

Evening 77:7–11
Will the LORD cast me off for ever?
will he no more show his favor?
Has his loving-kindness come to an end for ever?
has his promise failed for evermore?
Has God forgotten to be gracious?
has he, in his anger, withheld his compassion?
And I said, "My grief is this:
the right hand of the Most High has lost its power."
I will remember the works of the LORD,
and call to mind your wonders of old time.

What role does remembering play in your spiritual life?

June 28 ❀ Comfort

Morning 69:22–23
Reproach has broken my heart, and it cannot be healed;
I looked for sympathy, but there was none,
for comforters, but I could find no one.
They gave me gall to eat,
and when I was thirsty, they gave me vinegar to drink.

When you feel comfortless, what effect does it have on you to recall the times Jesus felt comfortless?

Evening 121:5–6
The Lord himself watches over you;
the Lord is your shade at your right hand,
So that the sun shall not strike you by day,
nor the moon by night.

Take the knowledge that God watches over you into your sleep.

June 29 ❀ Signs

Morning 18:3–5
I will call upon the Lord,
and so shall I be saved from my enemies.
The breakers of death rolled over me,
and the torrents of oblivion made me afraid.
The cords of hell entangled me,
and the snares of death were set for me.

What are some times in your life when you felt "the breakers of death" and "the torrents of oblivion"?

Evening 86:16–17
Turn to me and have mercy upon me;
give your strength to your servant;
and save the child of your handmaid.
Show me a sign of your favor,
so that those who hate me may see it and be ashamed;
because you, O Lord, have helped me and comforted me.

How does it feel—infantalizing? liberating? cozy?—to realize that you are a child of God?

June 30 ✿ Praise

Morning 68:33–36
Sing to God, O kingdoms of the earth;
sing praises to the LORD.
He rides in the heavens, the ancient heavens;
he sends forth his voice, his mighty voice.
Ascribe power to God;
his majesty is over Israel;
his strength is in the skies.
How wonderful is God in his holy places!
the God of Israel giving strength and power to his people!
Blessed be God!

Picture a God who gallops throughout creation, and who prances in your life this day.

Evening 130:4–5
I wait for the LORD; my soul waits for him;
in his word is my hope.
My soul waits for the LORD,
more than watchmen for the morning,
more than watchmen for the morning.

Fill in the blank: My soul waits for the Lord more than _____.

JULY

July 1 ❀ Favor

Morning 51:19–20
Be favorable and gracious to Zion,
and rebuild the walls of Jerusalem.
Then you will be pleased with the appointed sacrifices,
with burnt-offerings and oblations;
then shall they offer young bullocks upon your altar.

What do you think pleases God?

Evening 140:1–3
Deliver me, O LORD, from evildoers;
protect me from the violent,
Who devise evil in their hearts
and stir up strife all day long.
They have sharpened their tongues like a serpent;
adder's poison is under their lips.

Allow God to settle the strife that you have experienced today.

July 2 ❀ Malice

Morning 94:1–2
O LORD God of vengeance,
O God of vengeance, show yourself
Rise up, O Judge of the world;
give the arrogant their just deserts.

Do you believe that God is a God of vengeance?

Evening 7:15–18
Look at those who are in labor with wickedness,
who conceive evil, and give birth to a lie.
They dig a pit and make it deep
and fall into the hole that they have made.
Their malice turns back upon their own head;

their violence falls on their own scalp.
I will bear witness that the LORD is righteous;
I will praise the Name of the Lord Most High.

Pray for those whom you know who birth wickedness and who have
entrapped themselves with their malice.

July 3 ❈ Embodiment

Morning 147:5–6
Great is our LORD and mighty in power;
there is no limit to his wisdom.
The LORD lifts up the lowly,
but casts the wicked to the ground.

Invite God's unlimited wisdom into your life today.

Evening 22:14–15
I am poured out like water;
all my bones are out of joint;
my heart within my breast is melting wax.
My mouth is dried out like a pot-sherd;
my tongue sticks to the roof of my mouth;
and you have laid me in the dust of the grave.

Describe to God how you feel in your body this night.

July 4 ❈ Liberty

Morning 147:13–16
Worship the LORD, O Jerusalem;
praise your God, O Zion;
For he has strengthened the bars of your gates;
he has blessed your children within you.
He has established peace on your borders;
he satisfies you with the finest wheat.
He sends out his command to the earth,
and his word runs very swiftly.

How do you feel God has blessed the United States?

Evening 119:44–48
I shall continue to keep your law;
I shall keep it for ever and ever.

I will walk at liberty,
because I study your commandments.
I will tell of your decrees before kings
and will not be ashamed.
I delight in your commandments,
which I have always loved.
I will lift up my hands to your commandments,
and I will meditate on your statutes.

Meditate on the similarities and differences between civil laws and God's laws.

July 5 ❀ Preservation

Morning 121:7–8
The LORD shall preserve you from all evil;
it is he who shall keep you safe.
The LORD shall watch over your going out and your coming in,
from this time forth for evermore.

Realize that you live in God's safety.

Evening 115:14–18
May the LORD increase you more and more,
you and your children after you.
May you be blessed by the LORD,
the maker of heaven and earth.
The heaven of heavens is the LORD's,
but he entrusted the earth to its peoples.
The dead do not praise the LORD,
nor all those who go down into silence;
But we will bless the LORD,
from this time forth for evermore.
Hallelujah!

Do you believe that the dead do not praise God? What are the implications of your beliefs?

July 6 ❀ Assisting

Morning 102:19–22
For the LORD looked down from his holy place on high;
from the heavens he beheld the earth;

That he might hear the groan of the captive
and set free those condemned to die;
That they may declare in Zion the Name of the LORD,
and his praise in Jerusalem;
When the peoples are gathered together,
and the kingdoms also, to serve the LORD.

How can you help God hear the groan of the captive?

Evening 48:7–9
As we have heard, so have we seen,
in the city of the LORD *of hosts, in the city of our God;*
God has established her for ever.
We have waited in silence on your loving-kindness, O God,
in the midst of your temple.
Your praise, like your Name, O God, reaches to the world's end;
your right hand is full of justice.

Sleep in God's right hand, full of justice.

July 7 ✿ Silence

Morning 68:4–5
Sing to God, sing praises to his Name;
exalt him who rides upon the heavens;
YAHWEH *is his Name, rejoice before him!*
Father of orphans, defender of widows,
God in his holy habitation!

Once before each meal today, silently list reasons to praise God.

Evening 39:1–4
I said, "I will keep watch upon my ways,
so that I do not offend with my tongue.
I will put a muzzle on my mouth
while the wicked are in my presence."
So I held my tongue and said nothing;
I refrained from rash words;
but my pain became unbearable.
My heart was hot within me;
while I pondered, the fire burst into flame;
I spoke out with my tongue.

Review your words this day with God.

July 8 ❀ Bequest

Morning 49:9–10

For we see that the wise die also;
like the dull and stupid they perish
and leave their wealth to those who come after them.
Their graves shall be their homes for ever,
their dwelling places from generation to generation,
though they call the lands after their own names.

What kind of wealth will you leave behind?

Evening 67:1–4

May God be merciful to us and bless us,
show us the light of his countenance and come to us.
Let your ways be known upon earth,
your saving health among all nations.
Let the peoples praise you, O God;
let all the peoples praise you.
Let the nations be glad and sing for joy,
for you judge the peoples with equity
and guide all the nations upon earth.

For what acts of mercy and blessings do you praise God this night?

July 9 ❀ Presence

Morning 83:1–3

O God, do not be silent;
do not keep still nor hold your peace, O God;
For your enemies are in tumult,
and those who hate you have lifted up their heads.
They take secret counsel against your people
and plot against those whom you protect.

What makes people enemies of God?

Evening 103:20–22

Bless the LORD, you angels of his,
you mighty ones who do his bidding,
and hearken to the voice of his word.
Bless the LORD, all you his hosts,
you ministers of his who do his will.

Bless the LORD, all you works of his,
in all places of his dominion;
bless the LORD, O my soul.

Bless the Lord, knowing you are always in the presence of the Lord.

July 10 ❀ Trust

Morning 76:7–9
What terror you inspire!
who can stand before you when you are angry?
From heaven you pronounced judgment;
the earth was afraid and was still;
When God rose up to judgment
and to save all the oppressed of the earth.

Remember God's interest in the oppressed.

Evening 116:9–11
I believed, even when I said,
"I have been brought very low."
In my distress I said, "No one can be trusted."
How shall I repay the LORD
for all the good things he has done for me?
I will lift up the cup of salvation
and call upon the Name of the LORD.

How does your experience of trust with people color your experience of trust with God?

July 11 ❀ Words

Morning 15:5–7
He has sworn to do no wrong
and does not take back his word.
He does not give his money in hope of gain,
nor does he take a bribe against the innocent.
Whoever does these things
shall never be overthrown.

Resolve to keep your word today.

Evening 52:4–5
You love all words that hurt,

O you deceitful tongue.
Oh, that God would demolish you utterly,
topple you, and snatch you from your dwelling,
and root you out of the land of the living!

Hand over to God the words that hurt you today.

July 12 ❀ Truth

Morning 24:3–4
"Who can ascend the hill of the LORD?
and who can stand in his holy place?"
"Those who have clean hands and a pure heart,
who have not pledged themselves to falsehood,
nor sworn by what is a fraud."

Pledge yourself to truth.

Evening 9:13–14
Have pity on me, O LORD;
see the misery I suffer from those who hate me,
O you who lift me up from the gate of death;
So that I may tell of all your praises
and rejoice in your salvation
in the gates of the city of Zion.

Invite God to see your misery tonight so you may praise God in the morning.

July 13 ❀ Right Action

Morning 75:4–7
"I will say to the boasters, 'Boast no more,'
and to the wicked, 'Do not toss your horns;
Do not toss your horns so high,
nor speak with a proud neck.'"
For judgment is neither from the east nor from the west,
nor yet from the wilderness or the mountains.
It is God who judges;
he puts down one and lifts up another.

No need to respond to boasts.

Evening 122:6–9
Pray for the peace of Jerusalem:
"May they prosper who love you.
Peace be within your walls
and quietness within your towers.
For my brethren and companions' sake,
pray for your prosperity.
Because of the house of the Lord our God,
I will seek to do you good."

Pray for peace in the Middle East.

July 14 ❀ Strength

Morning 108:7–10
God spoke from his holy place and said,
"I will exult and parcel out Shechem;
I will divide the valley of Succoth.
Gilead is mine and Manasseh is mine;
Ephraim is my helmet and Judah my scepter.
Moab is my washbasin,
on Edom I throw down my sandal to claim it,
and over Philistia will I shout in triumph."
Who will lead me into the strong city?
who will bring me into Edom?

Ask God to bring you into a place of strength.

Evening 38:9–10
O LORD, you know all my desires,
and my sighing is not hidden from you.
My heart is pounding, my strength has failed me,
and the brightness of my eyes is gone from me.

God can replace anxiety with strength.

July 15 ❀ Emotion

Morning 89:38–40
But you have cast off and rejected your anointed;
you have become enraged at him.
You have broken your covenant with your servant,
defiled his crown, and hurled it to the ground.

You have breached all his walls
and laid his strongholds in ruins.

With whom do you feel God is enraged this day?

Evening 71:21–24
You strengthen me more and more;
you enfold and comfort me,
Therefore I will praise you upon the lyre for your faithfulness, O my God;
I will sing to you with the harp, O Holy One of Israel.
My lips will sing with joy when I play to you,
and so will my soul, which you have redeemed.
My tongue will proclaim your righteousness all day long,
for they are ashamed and disgraced who sought to do me harm.

How do you best express gratitude to God?

July 16 ✤ Tools

Morning 62:3–5
How long will you assail me to crush me,
all of you together,
as if you were a leaning fence, a toppling wall?
They seek only to bring me down from my place of honor;
lies are their chief delight.
They bless with their lips,
but in their hearts they curse.

When others are hypocritical, you can pray for discernment, endurance, discretion—and the ability to avoid hypocrisy in yourself.

Evening 6:10
All my enemies shall be confounded and quake with fear;
they shall turn back and suddenly be put to shame.

Visualize all the habits that attack your spirit turning from you in shame.

July 17 ✤ Innocence

Morning 26:6–7
I will wash my hands in innocence, O LORD,
that I may go in procession round your altar,
Singing aloud a song of thanksgiving

and recounting all your wonderful deeds.

Begin this day knowing that God grants you innocence.

Evening 4:3–5
Know that the LORD does wonders for the faithful;
when I call upon the LORD, he will hear me.
Tremble, then, and do not sin;
speak to your heart in silence upon your bed.
Offer the appointed sacrifices
and put your trust in the LORD.

God brings compassion into conversations between your heart and yourself.

July 18 ❀ Power

Morning 44:6–7
For I do not rely on my bow,
and my sword does not give me the victory.
Surely, you gave us victory over our adversaries
and put those who hate us to shame.

Realize that God is the strongest weapon against evil.

Evening 104:32–35
May the glory of the LORD endure for ever;
may the LORD rejoice in all his works.
He looks at the earth and it trembles;
he touches the mountains and they smoke.
I will sing to the LORD as long as I live;
I will praise my God while I have my being.
May these words of mine please him;
I will rejoice in the LORD.

How have you experienced God's power in your life today?

July 19 ❀ Fruits

Morning 92:12–14
Those who are planted in the house of the LORD
shall flourish in the courts of our God;
They shall still bear fruit in old age;

they shall be green and succulent;
That they may show how upright the Lord *is,*
my Rock, in whom there is no fault.

What kinds of fruit will you bear today?

Evening 67:5–7
Let the peoples praise you, O God;
let all the peoples praise you.
The earth has brought forth her increase;
may God, our own God, give us his blessing.
May God give us his blessing,
and may all the ends of the earth stand in awe of him.

Recall some of the earth's fruits that you have enjoyed today.

July 20 ❀ Covenant

Morning 74:17–19
Remember, O Lord, *how the enemy scoffed,*
how a foolish people despised your Name.
Do not hand over the life of your dove to wild beasts;
never forget the lives of your poor.
Look upon your covenant;
the dark places of the earth are haunts of violence.

Pray for that which you believe disappoints God today.

Evening 97:7–9
Confounded be all who worship carved images
and delight in false gods!
Bow down before him, all you gods.
Zion hears and is glad, and the cities of Judah rejoice,
because of your judgments, O Lord.
For you are the Lord,
most high over all the earth;
you are exalted far above all gods.

In what falsity have you delighted today?

July 21 ❀ God's Senses

Morning 11:5
His eyes behold the inhabited world;

his piercing eye weighs our worth.

How do you look in the eyes of God?

Evening 55:10–12
Swallow them up, O LORD;
confound their speech;
for I have seen violence and strife in the city.
Day and night the watchmen make their rounds upon her walls,
but trouble and misery are in the midst of her.
There is corruption at her heart;
her streets are never free of oppression and deceit.

What have you seen this day that you ask God to swallow up?

July 22 ❀ Nobility

Morning 45:1–2
My heart is stirring with a noble song;
let me recite what I have fashioned for the king;
my tongue shall be the pen of a skilled writer.
You are the fairest of men;
grace flows from your lips,
because God has blessed you for ever.

Offer to God the stirrings of your heart.

Evening 47:9–10
The nobles of the peoples have gathered together
with the people of the God of Abraham.
The rulers of the earth belong to God,
and he is highly exalted.

No matter the circumstances of our birth, we belong to God.

July 23 ❀ Progeny

Morning 128:1–4
Happy are they all who fear the LORD,
and who follow in his ways!
You shall eat the fruit of your labor;
happiness and prosperity shall be yours.
Your wife shall be like a fruitful vine within your house,
your children like olive shoots round about your table.

The man who fears the Lord
shall thus indeed be blessed.

Today, look for ways in which you are especially blessed because of your gender.

Evening 102:6–7
I have become like a vulture in the wilderness,
like an owl among the ruins.
I lie awake and groan;
I am like a sparrow, lonely on a house-top.

Describe your loneliness to God.

July 24 ✼ Beginnings and Endings

Morning 119:73–75
Your hands have made me and fashioned me;
give me understanding, that I may learn your commandments.
Those who fear you will be glad when they see me,
because I trust in your word.
I know, O LORD, that your judgments are right
and that in faithfulness you have afflicted me.

Seek God's understanding.

Evening 59:13–14
For the sins of their mouths, for the words of their lips,
for the cursing and lies that they utter,
let them be caught in their pride.
Make an end of them in your wrath;
make an end of them, and they shall be no more.

Give those who hurt you—and the world—to God.

July 25 ✼ Groaning

Morning 38:5–8
My wounds stink and fester
by reason of my foolishness.
I am utterly bowed down and prostrate;
I go about in mourning all the day long.
My loins are filled with searing pain;
there is no health in my body.

I am utterly numb and crushed;
I wail, because of the groaning of my heart.

Pray for those who awaken to depression.

Evening 119:39–40
Turn away the reproach which I dread,
because your judgments are good.
Behold, I long for your commandments;
in your righteousness preserve my life.

Pray for forgiveness.

July 26 ✤ Discernment

Morning 53:1–2
The fool has said in his heart, "There is no God."
All are corrupt and commit abominable acts;
there is none who does any good.
God looks down from heaven upon us all,
to see if there is any who is wise,
if there is one who seeks after God.

Seek only that which it is wise to seek.

Evening 54:1–3
Save me, O God, by your Name;
in your might, defend my cause.
Hear my prayer, O God;
give ear to the words of my mouth.
For the arrogant have risen up against me,
and the ruthless have sought my life,
those who have no regard for God.

What causes do you wish God to defend?

July 27 ✤ Friendship

Morning 25:13–14
The LORD is a friend to those who fear him
and will show them his covenant.
My eyes are ever looking to the LORD,
for he shall pluck my feet out of the net.

Keep your eyes on God's friendship today.

Evening 85:10–13
Mercy and truth have met together;
righteousness and peace have kissed each other.
Truth shall spring up from the earth,
and righteousness shall look down from heaven.
The Lord will indeed grant prosperity,
and our land will yield its increase.
Righteousness shall go before him,
and peace shall be a pathway for his feet.

Recall when you saw mercy and truth, righteousness and peace, together today.

July 28 ❀ Satisfaction

Morning 104:25
O Lord, how manifold are your works!
in wisdom you have made them all;
the earth is full of your creatures.

What will you create this day?

Evening 17:14–16
Deliver me, O Lord, by your hand
from those whose portion in life is this world;
Whose bellies you fill with your treasure,
who are well supplied with children
and leave their wealth to their little ones.
But at my vindication I shall see your face;
when I awake, I shall be satisfied, beholding your likeness.

Look forward to complete satisfaction.

July 29 ❀ Water

Morning 93:4–6
The waters have lifted up, O Lord,
the waters have lifted up their voice;
the waters have lifted up their pounding waves.
Mightier than the sound of many waters,
mightier than the breakers of the sea,
mightier is the Lord who dwells on high.
Your testimonies are very sure,

and holiness adorns your house, O LORD,
for ever and for evermore.

Listen for the voice of God in water.

Evening 102:8–10
My enemies revile me all day long,
and those who scoff at me have taken an oath against me.
For I have eaten ashes for bread
and mingled my drink with weeping.
Because of your indignation and wrath
you have lifted me up and thrown me away.

Have you ever felt that God threw you away?

July 30 ✾ Battle

Morning 18:13–16
From the brightness of his presence, through the clouds,
burst hailstones and coals of fire.
The LORD thundered out of heaven;
the Most High uttered his voice.
He loosed his arrows and scattered them;
he hurled thunderbolts and routed them.
The beds of the seas were uncovered,
and the foundations of the world laid bare,
at your battle cry, O LORD,
at the blast of the breath of your nostrils.

Notice God's battle cries today.

Evening 88:1–3
O LORD, my God, my Savior,
by day and night I cry to you.
Let my prayer enter into your presence;
incline your ear to my lamentation.
For I am full of trouble;
my life is at the brink of the grave.

God will do battle for you.

July 31 ❀ Integrity

Morning 111:4–6

He makes his marvelous works to be remembered;
the LORD is gracious and full of compassion.
He gives food to those who fear him;
he is ever mindful of his covenant.
He has shown his people the power of his works
in giving them the lands of the nations.

How mindful are *you* of God's covenant?

Evening 26:1–5

Give judgment for me, O LORD,
for I have lived with integrity;
I have trusted in the LORD and have not faltered.
Test me, O LORD, and try me;
examine my heart and my mind.
For your love is before my eyes;
I have walked faithfully with you.
I have not sat with the worthless,
nor do I consort with the deceitful.
I have hated the company of evildoers;
I will not sit down with the wicked.

How have you lived with integrity today?

AUGUST

August 1 ❀ Taking Sides

Morning 118:7–8

The LORD is at my side to help me;
I will triumph over those who hate me.
It is better to rely on the LORD
than to put any trust in flesh.

Notice God's reliability today.

Evening 139:18–21

Oh, that you would slay the wicked, O God!
You that thirst for blood, depart from me.
They speak despitefully against you;
your enemies take your Name in vain.
Do I not hate those, O LORD, who hate you?
and do I not loathe those who rise up against you?
I hate them with a perfect hatred;
they have become my own enemies.

How is it possible to be on the side of God?

August 2 ❀ Evildoers

Morning 94:3–5

How long shall the wicked, O LORD,
how long shall the wicked triumph?
They bluster in their insolence;
all evildoers are full of boasting.
They crush your people, O LORD,
and afflict your chosen nation.

Beware of those who bluster about you today.

Evening 71:10–12

For my enemies are talking against me,
and those who lie in wait for my life take counsel together.

They say, "God has forsaken him;
go after him and seize him;
because there is none who will save."
O God, be not far from me;
come quickly to help me, O my God.

Give your enemies to God.

August 3 ❀ Delighting in Sound

Morning 33:1–4
Rejoice in the LORD, *you righteous;*
it is good for the just to sing praises.
Praise the LORD *with the harp;*
play to him upon the psaltery and lyre.
Sing for him a new song;
sound a fanfare with all your skill upon the trumpet.
For the word of the LORD *is right,*
and all his works are sure.

Listen for sounds that bring you closer to God today.

Evening 49:11–12
Even though honored, they cannot live for ever;
they are like the beasts that perish.
Such is the way of those who foolishly trust in themselves,
and the end of those who delight in their own words.

No need to envy the self-centered!

August 4 ❀ Safety

Morning 69:37–38
For God will save Zion and rebuild the cities of Judah;
they shall live there and have it in possession.
The children of his servants will inherit it,
and those who love his Name will dwell therein.

Be mindful of future generations today.

Evening 31:19–20
How great is your goodness, O Lord!
which you have laid up for those who fear you;
which you have done in the sight of all

for those who put their trust in you.
You hide them in the covert of your presence from those who slander them;
you keep them in your shelter from the strife of tongues.

Imagine God as your armor against any words that hurt you today.

August 5 ❀ Hope

Morning 38:14–15
But I am like the deaf who do not hear,
like those who are mute and do not open their mouth.
I have become like one who does not hear
and from whose mouth comes no defense.
For in you, O LORD, have I fixed my hope;
you will answer me, O LORD my God.

Resolve to listen and speak to God today.

Evening 25:10–12
For your Name's sake, O LORD,
forgive my sin, for it is great.
Who are they who fear the LORD?
he will teach them the way that they should choose.
They shall dwell in prosperity,
and their offspring shall inherit the land.

What do you think comes to you when you give your sins to God?

August 6 ❀ The Transfiguration
(See Luke 9:28–36)

Morning 99:6–7
Moses and Aaron among his priests,
and Samuel among those who call upon his Name,
they called upon the LORD, and he answered them.
He spoke to them out of the pillar of cloud;
they kept his testimonies and the decree that he gave them.

Recall the times when you have felt the Lord transfigured your life.

Evening 99:8–9
"O LORD our God, you answered them indeed;
you were a God who forgave them,

yet punished them for their evil deeds."
Proclaim the greatness of the LORD our God
and worship him upon his holy hill;
for the LORD our God is the Holy One.

What reasons did today give you to proclaim the greatness of God?

August 7 ❁ Life

Morning 33:10–11
The LORD brings the will of the nations to naught;
he thwarts the designs of the peoples.
But the LORD's will stands fast for ever,
and the designs of his heart from age to age.

What design does God desire for your life?

Evening 49:13–15
Like a flock of sheep they are destined to die;
Death is their shepherd;
they go down straightway to the grave.
Their form shall waste away,
and the land of the dead shall be their home.
But God will ransom my life;
he will snatch me from the grasp of death.

Meditate on making life your shepherd.

August 8 ❁ Time

Morning 19:5–6
In the deep has he set a pavilion for the sun;
it comes forth like a bridegroom out of his chamber;
it rejoices like a champion to run its course.
It goes forth from the uttermost edge of the heavens
and runs about to the end of it again;
nothing is hidden from its burning heat.

God's creation is all around you throughout the day and the seasons.

Evening 148:3–6
Praise him, sun and moon;
praise him, all you shining stars.
Praise him, heaven of heavens,

and you waters above the heavens.
*Let them praise the Name of the L*ORD*;*
for he commanded, and they were created.
He made them stand fast for ever and ever;
he gave them a law which shall not pass away.

Meditate on God's eternal laws.

August 9 ✿ Battle

Morning 5:5–7
Braggarts cannot stand in your sight;
you hate all those who work wickedness.
You destroy those who speak lies;
*the bloodthirsty and deceitful, O L*ORD*, you abhor.*
But as for me, through the greatness of your mercy I will go into your house;
I will bow down toward your holy temple in awe of you.

Do not allow braggarts to intimidate you.

Evening 7:13–14
If they will not repent, God will whet his sword;
he will bend his bow and make it ready.
He has prepared his weapons of death;
he makes his arrows shafts of fire.

With what weapons do you think God does battle?

August 10 ✿ Amen

Morning 115:3–8
Our God is in heaven;
whatever he wills to do he does.
Their idols are silver and gold,
the work of human hands.
They have mouths, but they cannot speak;
eyes have they, but they cannot see;
They have ears, but they cannot hear;
noses, but they cannot smell;
They have hands, but they cannot feel;
feet, but they cannot walk;
they make no sound with their throat.
Those who make them are like them,

and so are all who put their trust in them.
Notice how your creations affect you.

Evening 72:18–19
Blessed be the Lord GOD, the God of Israel,
who alone does wondrous deeds!
And blessed be his glorious Name for ever!
and may all the earth be filled with his glory.
Amen. Amen.

"Amen" is Hebrew for "so be it." To what event in your life do you say
"Amen" this evening?

August 11 ❁ Embodiment

Morning 35:10
My very bones will say, "LORD, who is like you?
You deliver the poor from those who are too strong for them,
the poor and needy from those who rob them."
How do you feel God in your body?

Evening 84:10–12
For the LORD God is both sun and shield;
he will give grace and glory;
No good thing will the LORD withhold
from those who walk with integrity.
O LORD of hosts,
happy are they who put their trust in you!
Allow your body to relax, trusting in God's grace and glory.

August 12 ❁ Anger

Morning 64:5–6
They hold fast to their evil course;
they plan how they may hide their snares.
They say, "Who will see us?
who will find out our crimes?
we have thought out a perfect plot."
Beware of those who plot evil.

Evening 109:5–7
Set a wicked man against him,
and let an accuser stand at his right hand.
When he is judged, let him be found guilty,
and let his appeal be in vain.
Let his days be few,
and let another take his office.

What do you believe God desires for those who are wicked?

August 13 ❀ Bowing to the Lord

Morning 2:3–5
"Let us break their yoke," they say;
"let us cast off their bonds from us."
He whose throne is in heaven is laughing;
the LORD *has them in derision.*
Then he speaks to them in his wrath,
and his rage fills them with terror.

What do you think makes God laugh?

Evening 22:25–26
The poor shall eat and be satisfied,
and those who seek the LORD *shall praise him:*
"May your heart live for ever!"
All the ends of the earth shall remember and turn to the LORD,
and all the families of the nations shall bow before him.

Recall the times you have turned to the Lord today.

August 14 ❀ Refuge

Morning 71:1–4
In you, O LORD, *have I taken refuge;*
let me never be ashamed.
In your righteousness, deliver me and set me free;
incline your ear to me and save me.
Be my strong rock, a castle to keep me safe;
you are my crag and my stronghold.
Deliver me, my God, from the hand of the wicked,
from the clutches of the evildoer and the oppressor.

Seek to find freedom in God today.

Evening 36:10–12

Continue your loving-kindness to those who know you,
and your favor to those who are true of heart.
Let not the foot of the proud come near me,
nor the hand of the wicked push me aside.
See how they are fallen, those who work wickedness!
they are cast down and shall not be able to rise.

How have you continued your loving–kindness today?

August 15 ❈ Feast Day of St. Mary the Virgin
(See Luke 1:46–55)

Morning 34:11–14

Come, children, and listen to me;
I will teach you the fear of the LORD.
Who among you loves life
and desires long life to enjoy prosperity?
Keep your tongue from evil-speaking
and your lips from lying words.
Turn from evil and do good;
seek peace and pursue it.

Seek peace and pursue it today.

Evening 71:19–20

Your righteousness, O God, reaches to the heavens;
you have done great things;
who is like you, O God?
You have showed me great troubles and adversities,
but you will restore my life
and bring me up again from the deep places of the earth.

Recall Mary's troubles, adversities, and joys.

August 16 ❈ Authority

Morning 52:1–3

You tyrant, why do you boast of wickedness
against the godly all day long?
You plot ruin;
your tongue is like a sharpened razor,

O worker of deception.
You love evil more than good
and lying more than speaking the truth.

Carry the knowledge that tongues can be sharpened razors with you today.

Evening 61:6–8
Add length of days to the king's life;
let his years extend over many generations.
Let him sit enthroned before God for ever;
bid love and faithfulness watch over him.
So will I always sing the praise of your Name,
and day by day I will fulfill my vows.

Thank God for those who use their authority wisely.

August 17 ❀ Confidence

Morning 57:2–3
I will call upon the Most High God,
the God who maintains my cause.
He will send from heaven and save me;
he will confound those who trample upon me;
God will send forth his love and his faithfulness.

Remember that, as your sustainer, God maintains your cause.

Evening 104:26–29
Yonder is the great and wide sea
with its living things too many to number,
creatures both small and great.
There move the ships,
and there is that Leviathan,
which you have made for the sport of it.
All of them look to you
to give them their food in due season.
You give it to them; they gather it;
you open your hand, and they are filled with good things.

What have you seen today that you think God created for the sport of it?

August 18 ❁ God in Charge

Morning 48:1–3

Great is the LORD, and highly to be praised;
in the city of our God is his holy hill.
Beautiful and lofty, the joy of all the earth, is the hill of Zion,
the very center of the world and the city of the great King.
God is in her citadels;
he is known to be her sure refuge.

Carry the image of God at the center of the world today.

Evening 124:2–5

If the LORD had not been on our side,
when enemies rose up against us;
Then would they have swallowed us up alive
in their fierce anger toward us;
Then would the waters have overwhelmed us
and the torrent gone over us;
Then would the raging waters
have gone right over us.

How did God prevent you from feeling overwhelmed today?

August 19 ❁ Patience

Morning 71:12–14

O God, be not far from me;
come quickly to help me, O my God.
Let those who set themselves against me be put to shame and be disgraced;
let those who seek to do me evil be covered with scorn and reproach.
But I shall always wait in patience,
and shall praise you more and more.

What role does patience play in the drama of being hurt?

Evening 26:11–12

As for me, I will live with integrity;
redeem me, O LORD, and have pity on me.
My foot stands on level ground;
in the full assembly I will bless the LORD.

Imagine that people from your life are fully assembled, and that you are blessing God.

August 20 ❀ Asking

Morning 2:8–10
Ask of me, and I will give you the nations for your inheritance
and the ends of the earth for your possession.
You shall crush them with an iron rod
and shatter them like a piece of pottery."
And now, you kings, be wise;
be warned, you rulers of the earth.

What do you intend to ask of God this day?

Evening 24:8–10
"Who is this King of glory?"
"The LORD, *strong and mighty,*
the Lord, mighty in battle."
Lift up your heads, O gates;
lift them high, O everlasting doors;
and the King of glory shall come in.
"Who is he, this King of glory?"
"The LORD *of hosts,*
he is the King of glory."

Ask yourself: "Who is he, this King of glory?"

August 21 ❀ Time

Morning 78:1–3
Hear my teaching, O my people;
incline your ears to the words of my mouth.
I will open my mouth in a parable;
I will declare the mysteries of ancient times.
That which we have heard and known,
and what our forefathers have told us,
we will not hide from their children.

Listen for God's mysteries today so that you can tell of them.

Evening 44:3
For they did not take the land by their sword,
nor did their arm win the victory for them;
but your right hand, your arm, and the light of your countenance,

because you favored them.
Recall a time today when God gave you victory.

August 22 ❀ Judgment

Morning 119:156–159
Great is your compassion, O LORD;
preserve my life, according to your judgments.
There are many who persecute and oppress me,
yet I have not swerved from your decrees.
I look with loathing at the faithless,
for they have not kept your word.
See how I love your commandments!
O LORD, in your mercy, preserve me.
What do you loathe?

Evening 11:6–8
The LORD weighs the righteous as well as the wicked,
but those who delight in violence he abhors.
Upon the wicked he shall rain coals of fire and burning sulphur;
a scorching wind shall be their lot.
For the LORD is righteous;
he delights in righteous deeds;
and the just shall see his face.
Imagine the experience of seeing God's face.

August 23 ❀ The Earth

Morning 83:12–15
Who said, "Let us take for ourselves
the fields of God as our possession."
O my God, make them like whirling dust
and like chaff before the wind;
Like fire that burns down a forest,
like the flame that sets mountains ablaze.
Drive them with your tempest
and terrify them with your storm.
Remember that the earth belongs to God.

Evening 96:5–6
As for all the gods of the nations, they are but idols;
but it is the LORD who made the heavens.
Oh, the majesty and magnificence of his presence!
Oh, the power and the splendor of his sanctuary!

Recall the most magnificent characteristic you noticed in God's earth today.

August 24 ❀ Order

Morning 104:22–24
The lions roar after their prey
and seek their food from God.
The sun rises, and they slip away
and lay themselves down in their dens.
Man goes forth to his work
and to his labor until the evening.

Recognize that you are laboring today in the timeframe that God has ordered.

Evening 148:1–2
Hallelujah!
Praise the LORD from the heavens;
praise him in the heights.
Praise him, all you angels of his;
praise him, all his host.

Praise the Lord wherever you are this night.

August 25 ❀ Shame

Morning 37:19–20
The LORD cares for the lives of the godly,
and their inheritance shall last for ever.
They shall not be ashamed in bad times,
and in days of famine they shall have enough.

Forgo shame today!

Evening 9:3–5
When my enemies are driven back,
they will stumble and perish at your presence.

For you have maintained my right and my cause;
you sit upon your throne judging right.
You have rebuked the ungodly and destroyed the wicked;
you have blotted out their name for ever and ever.

Have you felt God maintaining your cause or forgoing shame today?

August 26 ❀ Witness

Morning 68:7–8
O God, when you went forth before your people,
when you marched through the wilderness,
The earth shook, and the skies poured down rain,
at the presence of God, the God of Sinai,
at the presence of God, the God of Israel.

Where do you feel the presence of God most strongly?

Evening 54:5–7
Render evil to those who spy on me;
in your faithfulness, destroy them.
I will offer you a freewill sacrifice
and praise your Name, O LORD, for it is good.
For you have rescued me from every trouble,
and my eye has seen the ruin of my foes.

What ruin have you witnessed today?

August 27 ❀ God's Works

Morning 46:9–10
Come now and look upon the works of the LORD,
what awesome things he has done on earth.
It is he who makes war to cease in all the world;
he breaks the bow, and shatters the spear,
and burns the shields with fire.

Look for God's peaceful works today.

Evening 104:5–6
You have set the earth upon its foundations,
so that it never shall move at any time.
You covered it with the Deep as with a mantle;

the waters stood higher than the mountains.
Meditate on the infant earth.

August 28 ❀ Confession

Morning 18:8–9
The earth reeled and rocked;
the roots of the mountains shook;
they reeled because of his anger.
Smoke rose from his nostrils
and a consuming fire out of his mouth;
hot burning coals blazed forth from him.
How do you see God's anger expressed?

Evening 32:3–6
While I held my tongue, my bones withered away,
because of my groaning all day long.
For your hand was heavy upon me day and night;
my moisture was dried up as in the heat of summer.
Then I acknowledged my sin to you,
and did not conceal my guilt.
I said, "I will confess my transgressions to the LORD."
Then you forgave me the guilt of my sin.
How does confessing to God affect you?

August 29 ❀ Relationship

Morning 54:4
Behold, God is my helper;
it is the LORD who sustains my life.
Think of God as your helper today.

Evening 60:6–9
God spoke from his holy place and said:
"I will exult and parcel out Shechem;
I will divide the valley of Succoth.
Gilead is mine and Manasseh is mine;
Ephraim is my helmet and Judah my scepter.
Moab is my wash-basin,

on Edom I throw down my sandal to claim it,
and over Philistia will I shout in triumph."
Who will lead me into the strong city?
who will bring me into Edom?

Describe how you see the relationship between God and nations.

August 30 ❀ Law

Morning 40:9
In the roll of the book it is written concerning me:
"I love to do your will, O my God;
your law is deep in my heart."

Bring God's law into your actions today.

Evening 72:8–10
He shall rule from sea to sea,
and from the River to the ends of the earth.
His foes shall bow down before him,
and his enemies lick the dust.
The kings of Tarshish and of the isles shall pay tribute,
and the kings of Arabia and Saba offer gifts.

In what ways did you see God's enemies licking dust today?

August 31 ❀ Enemies

Morning 10:5–6
Their ways are devious at all times;
your judgments are far above out of their sight;
they defy all their enemies.
They say in their heart, "I shall not be shaken;
no harm shall happen to me ever."

Vow to keep God's will in your sight today.

Evening 31:4–5
Take me out of the net that they have secretly set for me,
for you are my tower of strength.
Into your hands I commend my spirit,
for you have redeemed me,
O LORD, O God of truth.

Ask God to release you from all nets you feel are set for you.

SEPTEMBER

September 1 ✿ Change

Morning 6:6–7
I grow weary because of my groaning;
every night I drench my bed
and flood my couch with tears.
My eyes are wasted with grief
and worn away because of all my enemies.

You may bring to God whatever emotion has drenched your sleep.

Evening 40:3
He put a new song in my mouth,
a song of praise to our God;
many shall see, and stand in awe,
and put their trust in the LORD.

What has given you reason to trust God today?

September 2 ✿ Refuge

Morning 104:17–19
The trees of the LORD are full of sap,
the cedars of Lebanon which he planted,
In which the birds build their nests,
and in whose tops the stork makes his dwelling.
The high hills are a refuge for the mountain goats,
and the stony cliffs for the rock badgers.

Notice the refuges God gives to you today.

Evening 27:2–4
When evildoers came upon me to eat up my flesh,
it was they, my foes and my adversaries, who stumbled and fell.
Though an army should encamp against me,
yet my heart shall not be afraid;
And though war should rise up against me,

yet will I put my trust in him.

Recall a time when your heart was, without good reason, unafraid.

September 3 ❀ Heritage

Morning 112:5–6

It is good for them to be generous in lending
and to manage their affairs with justice.
For they will never be shaken;
the righteous will be kept in everlasting remembrance.

Pledge to manage your affairs with justice today.

Evening 45:17–18

"In place of fathers, O king, you shall have sons;
you shall make them princes over all the earth.
I will make your name to be remembered
from one generation to another;
therefore nations will praise you for ever and ever."

Remember that what you leave behind is more important than your heritage.

September 4 ❀ Covenant

Morning 89:34–37

I will not break my covenant,
nor change what has gone out of my lips.
Once for all I have sworn by my holiness:
"I will not lie to David.
His line shall endure for ever
and his throne as the sun before me;
It shall stand fast for evermore like the moon,
the abiding witness in the sky."

Notice the ways God keeps promises today.

Evening 37:34–35

The wicked spy on the righteous
and seek occasion to kill them.
The LORD will not abandon them to their hand,
nor let them be found guilty when brought to trial.

Recall times today when God could have abandoned you but did not.

September 5 ❀ Guiding

Morning 32:9–10

"I will instruct you and teach you in the way that you should go;
I will guide you with my eye.
Do not be like horse or mule, which have no understanding;
who must be fitted with bit and bridle,
or else they will not stay near you."

How can you show understanding today?

Evening 69:7

Let not those who hope in you be put to shame through me, Lord GOD of hosts;
let not those who seek you be disgraced because of me, O God of Israel.

What kind of guide have you been today?

September 6 ❀ Solidity

Morning 22:20–21

Save me from the lion's mouth,
my wretched body from the horns of wild bulls.
I will declare your Name to my brethren;
in the midst of the congregation I will praise you.

How do you plan to praise God today in the congregation in which you find yourself?

Evening 97:1–2

The LORD is King;
let the earth rejoice;
let the multitude of the isles be glad.
Clouds and darkness are round about him,
righteousness and justice are the foundations of his throne.

What are your foundations?

September 7 ❀ Mercy

Morning 50:16–17

But to the wicked God says:
"Why do you recite my statutes,
and take my covenant upon your lips;

Since you refuse discipline,
and toss my words behind your back?"

Keep God's words in front of you.

Evening 123:4–5
Have mercy upon us, O LORD, have mercy,
for we have had more than enough of contempt,
Too much of the scorn of the indolent rich,
and of the derision of the proud.

If you have felt scorned today, ask for God's mercy on those who
showed you contempt; if you have scorned others today, ask for God's
mercy on yourself.

September 8 ❀ History

Morning 85:1–3
You have been gracious to your land, O LORD,
you have restored the good fortune of Jacob.
You have forgiven the iniquity of your people
and blotted out all their sins.
You have withdrawn all your fury
and turned yourself from your wrathful indignation.

Notice God's graciousness to you today.

Evening 136:13–16
Who divided the Red Sea in two,
for his mercy endures for ever;
And made Israel to pass through the midst of it,
for his mercy endures for ever;
But swept Pharaoh and his army into the Red Sea,
for his mercy endures for ever;
Who led his people through the wilderness,
for his mercy endures for ever.

How have you noticed God's mercy in your history?

September 9 ❀ Preservation

Morning 145:21–22
The LORD preserves all those who love him,
but he destroys all the wicked.

My mouth shall speak the praise of the LORD;
let all flesh bless his holy Name for ever and ever.

Speak the praise of the Lord today in as many ways and as often as possible.

Evening 111:1–3
Hallelujah!
I will give thanks to the LORD with my whole heart,
in the assembly of the upright, in the congregation.
Great are the deeds of the LORD!
they are studied by all who delight in them.
His work is full of majesty and splendor,
and his righteousness endures for ever.

Pray to understand God's righteousness better and better.

September 10 ❁ Evildoers

Morning 10:7–8
Their mouth is full of cursing, deceit, and oppression;
under their tongue are mischief and wrong.
They lurk in ambush in public squares
and in secret places they murder the innocent;
they spy out the helpless.

Remember that God sees those who do evil as well as those who do good.

Evening 10:9–11
They lie in wait, like a lion in a covert;
they lie in wait to seize upon the lowly;
they seize the lowly and drag them away in their net.
The innocent are broken and humbled before them;
the helpless fall before their power.
They say in their heart, "God has forgotten;
he hides his face; he will never notice."

Does it ever feel to you that God does not notice?

September 11 ❁ Evil Days

Morning 49:1–2
Hear this, all you peoples;

hearken, all you who dwell in the world,
you of high degree and low, rich and poor together.
My mouth shall speak of wisdom,
and my heart shall meditate on understanding.

God is the God of all people.

Evening 49:3–5
I will incline my ear to a proverb
and set forth my riddle upon the harp.
Why should I be afraid in evil days,
when the wickedness of those at my heels surrounds me,
The wickedness of those who put their trust in their goods,
and boast of their great riches?

Meditate on that which erases your fear.

September 12 ❀ Shouting

Morning 47:5
God has gone up with a shout,
the Lord with the sound of the ram's-horn.

Listen for God today.

Evening 30:8–11
Then you hid your face,
and I was filled with fear.
I cried to you, O Lord;
I pleaded with the Lord, saying,
"What profit is there in my blood, if I go down to the Pit?
will the dust praise you or declare your faithfulness?
Hear, O Lord, and have mercy upon me;
O Lord, be my helper."

Recall a time when you bargained with God.

September 13 ❀ Rage

Morning 119:53
I am filled with a burning rage,
because of the wicked who forsake your law.

Tend to your anger.

Evening 18:10–12
He parted the heavens and came down
with a storm cloud under his feet.
He mounted on cherubim and flew;
he swooped on the wings of the wind.
He wrapped darkness about him;
he made dark waters and thick clouds his pavilion.

God's pavilion is everywhere you are.

September 14 ❀ Holy Cross Day
(See Ephesians 2: 11–22)

Morning 98:1–2
Sing to the LORD *a new song,*
for he has done marvelous things.
With his right hand and his holy arm
has he won for himself the victory.

Each new day is an opportunity for a new song.

Evening 98:3–4
The LORD *has made known his victory;*
his righteousness has he openly shown in the sight of the nations.
He remembers his mercy and faithfulness to the house of Israel,
and all the ends of the earth have seen the victory of our God.

Recall a time in the course of this day when you saw God's victory.

September 15 ❀ Unity

Morning 148:11–12
Kings of the earth and all peoples,
princes and all rulers of the world;
Young men and maidens,
old and young together.

Notice what unites human beings today.

Evening 140:6–7
I have said to the LORD, *"You are my God;*
listen, O Lord, to my supplication.
O Lord GOD, *the strength of my salvation,*
you have covered my head in the day of battle.

How has conflict separated you from, and united you with, others today?

September 16 ❀ God's Presence

Morning 68:7–8
O God, when you went forth before your people,
when you marched through the wilderness,
The earth shook, and the skies poured down rain,
at the presence of God, the God of Sinai,
at the presence of God, the God of Israel.

Be on the look-out for God's presence today.

Evening 104:36–37
Let sinners be consumed out of the earth,
and the wicked be no more.
Bless the LORD, O my soul.
Hallelujah!

Imagine a world devoid of evil.

September 17 ❀ Seeking

Morning 24:5–6
They shall receive a blessing from the LORD
and a just reward from the God of their salvation."
Such is the generation of those who seek him,
of those who seek your face, O God of Jacob.

What does it mean to you to seek God's face?

Evening 90:7–9
For we consume away in your displeasure;
we are afraid because of your wrathful indignation.
Our iniquities you have set before you,
and our secret sins in the light of your countenance.
When you are angry, all our days are gone;
we bring our years to an end like a sigh.

Do you believe God's anger causes death?

September 18 ❦ God's Nature

Morning 46:1–4

God is our refuge and strength,
a very present help in trouble.
Therefore we will not fear, though the earth be moved,
and though the mountains be toppled into the depths of the sea;
Though its waters rage and foam,
and though the mountains tremble at its tumult.
The LORD of hosts is with us;
the God of Jacob is our stronghold.

What about God helps you overcome fear?

Evening 9:12

The Avenger of blood will remember them;
he will not forget the cry of the afflicted.

How does it make you feel to think of God as "the Avenger of blood?"

September 19 ❦ Eternal

Morning 10:17–19

The LORD is King for ever and ever;
the ungodly shall perish from his land.
The LORD will hear the desire of the humble;
you will strengthen their heart and your ears shall hear;
To give justice to the orphan and oppressed,
so that mere mortals may strike terror no more.

Focus on that which is eternal.

Evening 14:5–7

See how they tremble with fear,
because God is in the company of the righteous.
Their aim is to confound the plans of the afflicted,
but the LORD is their refuge.
Oh, that Israel's deliverance would come out of Zion!
when the LORD restores the fortunes of his people,
Jacob will rejoice and Israel be glad.

How have you felt God's company today?

September 20 ❦ Righteousness

Morning 58:8–11
Let them be like the snail that melts away,
like a stillborn child that never sees the sun.
Before they bear fruit, let them be cut down like a brier;
like thorns and thistles let them be swept away.
The righteous will be glad when they see the vengeance;
they will bathe their feet in the blood of the wicked.
And they will say,
"Surely, there is a reward for the righteous;
surely, there is a God who rules in the earth."

What do you think God desires for those who are not righteous?

Evening 40:10
I proclaimed righteousness in the great congregation;
behold, I did not restrain my lips;
and that, O LORD, you know.

What did your lips proclaim today?

September 21 ❦ Signs

Morning 75:1–3
We give you thanks, O God, we give you thanks,
calling upon your Name and declaring all your wonderful deeds.
"I will appoint a time," says God;
"I will judge with equity.
Though the earth and all its inhabitants are quaking,
I will make its pillars fast."

Look for signs of God's stability today.

Evening 101:5
Those who in secret slander their neighbors I will destroy;
those who have a haughty look and a proud heart I cannot abide.

What signs did your expressions give to others today?

September 22 ❀ Bowed

Morning 57:4–5
I lie in the midst of lions that devour the people;
their teeth are spears and arrows,
their tongue a sharp sword.
They have laid a net for my feet,
and I am bowed low;
they have dug a pit before me,
but have fallen into it themselves.

Keep in mind that people often trap themselves.

Evening 115:1–2
Not to us, O Lord, not to us,
but to your Name give glory;
because of your love and because of your faithfulness.
Why should the heathen say,
"Where then is their God?"

What does God's faithfulness have in common with your faithfulness?

September 23 ❀ Splendor

Morning 29:4–6
The voice of the Lord is a powerful voice;
the voice of the Lord is a voice of splendor.
The voice of the Lord breaks the cedar trees;
the Lord breaks the cedars of Lebanon;
He makes Lebanon skip like a calf,
and Mount Hermon like a young wild ox.

How does God sound to you?

Evening 12:7–8
O Lord, watch over us
and save us from this generation for ever.
The wicked prowl on every side,
and that which is worthless is highly prized by everyone.

What did you prize today?

September 24 ✸ Direction

Morning 38:19–22

Those who are my enemies without cause are mighty,
and many in number are those who wrongfully hate me.
Those who repay evil for good slander me,
because I follow the course that is right.
O LORD, do not forsake me;
be not far from me, O my God.
Make haste to help me,
O LORD of my salvation.

Ask God to help you follow the right course today.

Evening 55:25–26

For you will bring the bloodthirsty and deceitful
down to the pit of destruction, O God.
They shall not live out half their days,
but I will put my trust in you.

Do not be afraid to separate yourself from those who are deceitful.

September 25 ✸ Knowledge

Morning 59:4–6

Not because of any guilt of mine
they run and prepare themselves for battle.
Rouse yourself, come to my side, and see;
for you, LORD God of hosts, are Israel's God.
Awake, and punish all the ungodly;
show no mercy to those who are faithless and evil.

To what do you hope God will awaken?

Evening 73:10–12

And so the people turn to them
and find in them no fault.
They say, "How should God know?
is there knowledge in the Most High?"
So then, these are the wicked;
always at ease, they increase their wealth.

Do you believe God is all-knowing? How does this belief shape your daily actions?

September 26 ❀ Dwellings

Morning 26:8–10

Lord, I love the house in which you dwell
and the place where your glory abides.
Do not sweep me away with sinners,
nor my life with those who thirst for blood,
Whose hands are full of evil plots,
and their right hand full of bribes.

Make yourself hospitable to God's glory.

Evening 94:15–17

For judgment will again be just,
and all the true of heart will follow it.
Who rose up for me against the wicked?
who took my part against the evildoers?
If the Lord had not come to my help,
I should soon have dwelt in the land of silence.

How does God give you voice?

September 27 ❀ Evildoers

Morning 9: 6–8

As for the enemy, they are finished, in perpetual ruin,
their cities ploughed under, the memory of them perished;
But the Lord is enthroned for ever;
he has set up his throne for judgment.
It is he who rules the world with righteousness;
he judges the peoples with equity.

Explore your feelings about God's memory.

Evening 6:8–9

Depart from me, all evildoers,
for the Lord has heard the sound of my weeping.
The Lord has heard my supplication;
the Lord accepts my prayer.

Do you feel your prayers have been accepted today?

September 28 ❀ Malice

Morning 12:1–4
Help me, LORD, for there is no godly one left;
the faithful have vanished from among us.
Everyone speaks falsely with his neighbor;
with a smooth tongue they speak from a double heart.
Oh, that the LORD would cut off all smooth tongues,
and close the lips that utter proud boasts!
Those who say, "With our tongue will we prevail;
our lips are our own; who is lord over us?"

Beware of smooth tongues and double hearts today.

Evening 27:16
Deliver me not into the hand of my adversaries,
for false witnesses have risen up against me,
and also those who speak malice.

Realize that you are delivered into the hand of God.

September 29 ❀ Power

Morning 11:1–3
In the LORD have I taken refuge;
how then can you say to me,
"Fly away like a bird to the hilltop;
For see how the wicked bend the bow
and fit their arrows to the string,
to shoot from ambush at the true of heart.
When the foundations are being destroyed,
what can the righteous do?"

Well, what *can* the righteous do?

Evening 30:7
While I felt secure, I said,
"I shall never be disturbed.
You, LORD, with your favor, made me as strong as the mountains."

Fill in the blank: You, Lord, with your favor, made me as strong
as_____.

September 30 ❀ Recounting

Morning 78:4–5

We will recount to generations to come
the praiseworthy deeds and the power of the LORD,
and the wonderful works he has done.
He gave his decrees to Jacob
and established a law for Israel,
which he commanded them to teach their children.

What do you think is important for children to know?

Evening 78:6–8

That the generations to come might know,
and the children yet unborn;
that they in their turn might tell it to their children;
So that they might put their trust in God,
and not forget the deeds of God,
but keep his commandments;
And not be like their forefathers,
a stubborn and rebellious generation,
a generation whose heart was not steadfast,
and whose spirit was not faithful to God.

What gives you the most hope for children yet unborn?

OCTOBER

October 1 ❀ Heritage

Morning 16:5–6

O LORD, you are my portion and my cup;
it is you who uphold my lot.
My boundaries enclose a pleasant land;
indeed, I have a goodly heritage.

Remember that you bring your godly heritage into this day.

Evening 18:38–40

I pursue my enemies and overtake them;
I will not turn back till I have destroyed them.
I strike them down, and they cannot rise;
they fall defeated at my feet.
You have girded me with strength for the battle;
you have cast down my adversaries beneath me;
you have put my enemies to flight.

Take strength from the past.

October 2 ❀ Limits

Morning 104:7–9

At your rebuke they fled;
at the voice of your thunder they hastened away.
They went up into the hills and down to the valleys beneath,
to the places you had appointed for them.
You set the limits that they should not pass;
they shall not again cover the earth.

Although the psalm refers here to the limits God placed on "the waters," what other kinds of limits could it refer to?

Evening 76:4–6

How glorious you are!
more splendid than the everlasting mountains!

The strong of heart have been despoiled;
they sink into sleep;
none of the warriors can lift a hand.
At your rebuke, O God of Jacob,
both horse and rider lie stunned.

What stuns you about the limits God has created?

October 3 ❀ Springs

Morning 87:3–6
I count Egypt and Babylon among those who know me;
behold Philistia, Tyre, and Ethiopia:
in Zion were they born.
Of Zion it shall be said, "Everyone was born in her,
and the Most High himself shall sustain her."
The LORD *will record as he enrolls the peoples,*
"These also were born there."
The singers and the dancers will say,
"All my fresh springs are in you."

What fresh springs well in you today?

Evening 21:1–3
The king rejoices in your strength, O LORD;
how greatly he exults in your victory!
You have given him his heart's desire;
you have not denied him the request of his lips.
For you meet him with blessings of prosperity,
and set a crown of fine gold upon his head.

Which of your requests has God given you today?

October 4 ❀ Endurance

Morning 91:14–16
Because he is bound to me in love,
therefore will I deliver him;
I will protect him, because he knows my Name.
He shall call upon me, and I will answer him;
I am with him in trouble;
I will rescue him and bring him to honor.
With long life will I satisfy him,

and show him my salvation.
Know God's name and protection.

Evening 102:23–24
He has brought down my strength before my time;
he has shortened the number of my days;
And I said, "O my God,
do not take me away in the midst of my days;
your years endure throughout all generations."
Recall a moment in your life when your sense of the present collided with God's sense of the eternal.

October 5 ✿ Hope

Morning 33:16–17
There is no king that can be saved by a mighty army;
a strong man is not delivered by his great strength.
The horse is a vain hope for deliverance;
for all its strength it cannot save.
Hope in God.

Evening 147:1–4
Hallelujah!
How good it is to sing praises to our God!
how pleasant it is to honor him with praise!
The LORD rebuilds Jerusalem;
he gathers the exiles of Israel.
He heals the brokenhearted
and binds up their wounds.
He counts the number of the stars
and calls them all by their names.
How well do you think God knows you?

October 6 ✿ Restraint

Morning 119:101–103
I restrain my feet from every evil way,
that I may keep your word.
I do not shrink from your judgments,
because you yourself have taught me.

How sweet are your words to my taste!
they are sweeter than honey to my mouth.

Which of God's gifts will be sweetest to you today?

Evening 39:11–12
Take your affliction from me;
I am worn down by the blows of your hand.
With rebukes for sin you punish us;
like a moth you eat away all that is dear to us;
truly, everyone is but a puff of wind.

When bad things happen, do you tend to feel that you are being punished by God or are a victim of evil?

October 7 ❀ Faults

Morning 19:12
Who can tell how often he offends?
cleanse me from my secret faults.

Begin today with a confession of your secret faults so you can feel spiritually clean.

Evening 119:4–8
You laid down your commandments,
that we should fully keep them.
Oh, that my ways were made so direct
that I might keep your statutes!
Then I should not be put to shame,
when I regard all your commandments.
I will thank you with an unfeigned heart,
when I have learned your righteous judgments.
I will keep your statutes;
do not utterly forsake me.

When does the right way seem most obscure to you?

October 8 ❀ Remember

Morning 137:4–6
How shall we sing the LORD's song
upon an alien soil?
If I forget you, O Jerusalem,

let my right hand forget its skill.
Let my tongue cleave to the roof of my mouth
if I do not remember you,
if I do not set Jerusalem above my highest joy.

Sing of God today, no matter how alien your surroundings.

Evening 18:50
He multiplies the victories of his king;
he shows loving-kindness to his anointed,
to David and his descendants for ever.

How have you felt God's loving-kindness today?

October 9 ❀ Courage

Morning 45:3–5
Strap your sword upon your thigh, O mighty warrior,
in your pride and in your majesty.
Ride out and conquer in the cause of truth
and for the sake of justice.
Your right hand will show you marvelous things;
your arrows are very sharp, O mighty warrior.

What are the sharpest weapons you have against the injustice that most troubles you?

Evening 56:3–4
Whenever I am afraid,
I will put my trust in you.
In God, whose word I praise,
in God I trust and will not be afraid,
for what can flesh do to me?

Meditate on the limitations of the flesh.

October 10 ❀ Withered Heart

Morning 27:13–15
You have been my helper;
cast me not away;
do not forsake me, O God of my salvation.
Though my father and my mother forsake me,
the LORD will sustain me.

Show me your way, O Lord;
lead me on a level path, because of my enemies.

Work with God to turn your fear into trust.

Evening 102:4–5
My heart is smitten like grass and withered,
so that I forget to eat my bread.
Because of the voice of my groaning
I am but skin and bones.

Know that God hears your groaning.

October 11 ❀ Craving

Morning 78:29–30
So they ate and were well filled,
for he gave them what they craved.
But they did not stop their craving,
though the food was still in their mouths.

Is what you crave what God desires for you?

Evening 115:11–13
You who fear the Lord, trust in the Lord;
he is their help and their shield.
The Lord has been mindful of us, and he will bless us;
he will bless the house of Israel;
he will bless the house of Aaron;
He will bless those who fear the Lord,
both small and great together.

Is there any relationship between respect (fear) for the Lord and your
sense of the Lord as a shield in which you may trust?

October 12 ❀ Entanglement

Morning 131:1–2
O Lord, I am not proud;
I have no haughty looks.
I do not occupy myself with great matters,
or with things that are too hard for me.

What do you intend to hand over to God today?

Evening 119:61–62
Though the cords of the wicked entangle me,
I do not forget your law.
At midnight I will rise to give you thanks,
because of your righteous judgments.

If you find yourself awake in the middle of the night, spend some of the time thanking God for the blessings of the day.

October 13 ❁ Integrity

Morning 50:18–21
"When you see a thief, you make him your friend,
and you cast in your lot with adulterers.
You have loosed your lips for evil,
and harnessed your tongue to a lie.
You are always speaking evil of your brother
and slandering your own mother's son.
These things you have done, and I kept still,
and you thought that I am like you."

Be sure you demonstrate who you are.

Evening 139:22–23
Search me out, O God, and know my heart;
try me and know my restless thoughts.
Look well whether there be any wickedness in me
and lead me in the way that is everlasting.

Meditate on the way that is everlasting.

October 14 ❁ Strength

Morning 89:21
My hand will hold him fast
and my arm will make him strong.

Allow these words to give you strength today.

Evening 74:1–4
O God, why have you utterly cast us off?
why is your wrath so hot against the sheep of your pasture?
Remember your congregation that you purchased long ago,
the tribe you redeemed to be your inheritance,

and Mount Zion where you dwell.
Turn your steps toward the endless ruins;
the enemy has laid waste everything in your sanctuary.
Your adversaries roared in your holy place;
they set up their banners as tokens of victory.

Toward what do you desire God's steps to be turned?

October 15 ❦ Voices

Morning 29:8–9
The voice of the L*ORD* *makes the oak trees writhe*
and strips the forests bare.
And in the temple of the L*ORD*
all are crying, "Glory!"

Be attuned to God's glory today.

Evening 109:17–19
He put on cursing like a garment,
let it soak into his body like water
and into his bones like oil;
Let it be to him like the cloak which he wraps around himself,
and like the belt that he wears continually.
Let this be the recompense from the L*ORD* *to my accusers,*
and to those who speak evil against me.

What language do you put on like a garment?

October 16 ❦ Tests

Morning 22:18–19
Be not far away, O L*ORD;*
you are my strength; hasten to help me.
Save me from the sword,
my life from the power of the dog.

What power can overpower God?

Evening 66:7–11
Bless our God, you peoples;
make the voice of his praise to be heard;
Who holds our souls in life,

and will not allow our feet to slip.
For you, O God, have proved us;
you have tried us just as silver is tried.
You brought us into the snare;
you laid heavy burdens upon our backs.
You let enemies ride over our heads;
we went through fire and water;
but you brought us out into a place of refreshment.

Let your sleep be a place of refreshment.

October 17 ✲ Indignation

Morning 78:6–8
That the generations to come might know,
and the children yet unborn;
that they in their turn might tell it to their children;
So that they might put their trust in God,
and not forget the deeds of God,
but keep his commandments;
And not be like their forefathers,
a stubborn and rebellious generation,
a generation whose heart was not steadfast,
and whose spirit was not faithful to God.

How do you hope the new generation differs from your own?

Evening 69:24–26
Let the table before them be a trap
and their sacred feasts a snare.
Let their eyes be darkened, that they may not see,
and give them continual trembling in their loins.
Pour out your indignation upon them,
and let the fierceness of your anger overtake them.

No matter how fierce your rage, you can take it to God.

October 18 ✲ Awe

Morning 65:5–7
Awesome things will you show us in your righteousness,
O God of our salvation,

O Hope of all the ends of the earth
and of the seas that are far away.
You make fast the mountains by your power;
they are girded about with might.
You still the roaring of the seas,
the roaring of their waves,
and the clamor of the peoples.

Look for God in awesome sights today.

Evening 86:14–15
The arrogant rise up against me, O God,
and a band of violent men seeks my life;
they have not set you before their eyes.
But you, O LORD, are gracious and full of compassion,
slow to anger, and full of kindness and truth.

Meditate on any relationships you perceive between God and violence.

October 19 ❈ Gates

Morning 100:3–4
Enter his gates with thanksgiving;
go into his courts with praise;
give thanks to him and call upon his Name.
For the LORD is good;
his mercy is everlasting;
and his faithfulness endures from age to age.

What does it mean for faithfulness to endure from age to age?

Evening 77:18–20
The sound of your thunder was in the whirlwind;
your lightnings lit up the world;
the earth trembled and shook.
Your way was in the sea,
and your paths in the great waters,
yet your footsteps were not seen.
You led your people like a flock
by the hand of Moses and Aaron.

Where did you see God's ways today?

October 20 ❀ Persistent

Morning 39:7–8
We walk about like a shadow,
and in vain we are in turmoil;
we heap up riches and cannot tell who will gather them.
And now, what is my hope?
O LORD, my hope is in you.

Remember that much of your turmoil is in vain.

Evening 119:166–168
I have hoped for your salvation, O LORD,
and I have fulfilled your commandments.
I have kept your decrees
and I have loved them deeply.
I have kept your commandments and decrees,
for all my ways are before you.

Recall the ways you have kept and loved God's decrees today.

October 21 ❀ Inheritance

Morning 110:4
The LORD has sworn and he will not recant:
"You are a priest for ever after the order of Melchizedek."

What has God made *you* forever?

Evening 79:1–3
O God, the heathen have come into your inheritance;
they have profaned your holy temple;
they have made Jerusalem a heap of rubble.
They have given the bodies of your servants as food for the birds of the air,
and the flesh of your faithful ones to the beasts of the field.
They have shed their blood like water on every side of Jerusalem,
and there was no one to bury them.

What causes you to lament with God?

October 22 ❀ Invitations

Morning 118:9–10
It is better to rely on the LORD

than to put any trust in rulers.
All the ungodly encompass me;
in the name of the LORD I will repel them.

Realize that God is your shield.

Evening 40:7–8
In sacrifice and offering you take no pleasure
(you have given me ears to hear you);
Burnt-offering and sin-offering you have not required,
and so I said, "Behold, I come."

What do you think God requires?

October 23 ❈ Blessing

Morning 72:17
May his Name remain for ever
and be established as long as the sun endures;
may all the nations bless themselves in him and call him blessed.

Bless *yourself* in God.

Evening 122:1–4
I was glad when they said to me,
"Let us go to the house of the LORD."
Now our feet are standing
within your gates, O Jerusalem.
Jerusalem is built as a city
that is at unity with itself;
To which the tribes go up,
the tribes of the LORD,
the assembly of Israel,
to praise the Name of the LORD.

Meditate on the blessing of being at unity with yourself.

October 24 ❈ God's Favor

Morning 102:15–18
The nations shall fear your Name, O LORD,
and all the kings of the earth your glory.
For the LORD will build up Zion,
and his glory will appear.

He will look with favor on the prayer of the homeless;
he will not despise their plea.
Let this be written for a future generation,
so that a people yet unborn may praise the Lord.

Pray for the homeless.

Evening 44:8–10
Every day we gloried in God,
and we will praise your Name for ever.
Nevertheless, you have rejected and humbled us
and do not go forth with our armies.
You have made us fall back before our adversary,
and our enemies have plundered us.

Have you felt God was not on your side today?

October 25 ❀ Saving Acts

Morning 71:15–16
My mouth shall recount your mighty acts
and saving deeds all day long;
though I cannot know the number of them.
I will begin with the mighty works of the Lord GOD
I will recall your righteousness, yours alone.

Focus on God for a few minutes this morning and notice if that time affects your day.

Evening 38:16–18
For I said, "Do not let them rejoice at my expense,
those who gloat over me when my foot slips."
Truly, I am on the verge of falling,
and my pain is always with me.
I will confess my iniquity
and be sorry for my sin.

Falling into the arms of God is always safe.

October 26 ❀ Begotten

Morning 2:6–7
"I myself have set my king
upon my holy hill of Zion."

Let me announce the decree of the LORD:
he said to me, "You are my Son;
this day have I begotten you."

Try on the realization that God has begotten you.

Evening 149:6–9
Let the praises of God be in their throat
and a two-edged sword in their hand;
To wreak vengeance on the nations
and punishment on the peoples;
To bind their kings in chains
and their nobles with links of iron;
To inflict on them the judgment decreed;
this is glory for all his faithful people.
Hallelujah!

What does "glory" mean among faithful people?

October 27 ✤ Wisdom

Morning 39:5–6
LORD, *let me know my end and the number of my days,*
so that I may know how short my life is.
You have given me a mere handful of days,
and my lifetime is as nothing in your sight;
truly, even those who stand erect are but a puff of wind.

Look for that which is precious in life today.

Evening 139:1–4
LORD, *you have searched me out and known me;*
you know my sitting down and my rising up;
you discern my thoughts from afar.
You trace my journeys and my resting-places
and are acquainted with all my ways.
Indeed, there is not a word on my lips,
but you, O LORD, *know it altogether.*
You press upon me behind and before
and lay your hand upon me.

How do you feel about God knowing you so well?

October 28 ❀ Thanks

Morning 95:1–3
Come, let us sing to the L*ORD*;
let us shout for joy to the Rock of our salvation.
Let us come before his presence with thanksgiving
and raise a loud shout to him with psalms.
For the L*ORD* *is a great God,*
and a great King above all gods.

Give thanks for those who bring you joy.

Evening 104:13–16
You water the mountains from your dwelling on high;
the earth is fully satisfied by the fruit of your works.
You make grass grow for flocks and herds
and plants to serve mankind;
That they may bring forth food from the earth,
and wine to gladden our hearts,
Oil to make a cheerful countenance,
and bread to strengthen the heart.

Recall how food you have eaten today has gone beyond nourishing your body.

October 29 ❀ Freedom

Morning 31:7–8
I will rejoice and be glad because of your mercy;
for you have seen my affliction;
you know my distress.
You have not shut me up in the power of the enemy;
you have set my feet in an open place.

Recognize the open places in your life.

Evening 119:133–136
Steady my footsteps in your word;
let no iniquity have dominion over me.
Rescue me from those who oppress me,
and I will keep your commandments.
Let your countenance shine upon your servant

and teach me your statutes.
My eyes shed streams of tears,
because people do not keep your law.

What saddens you about the world?

October 30 ❀ Admonition

Morning 81:8–9
Hear, O my people, and I will admonish you:
O Israel, if you would but listen to me!
There shall be no strange god among you;
you shall not worship a foreign god.

God is knowable.

Evening 119:69–72
The proud have smeared me with lies,
but I will keep your commandments with my whole heart.
Their heart is gross and fat,
but my delight is in your law.
It is good for me that I have been afflicted,
that I might learn your statutes.
The law of your mouth is dearer to me
than thousands in gold and silver.

What have the afflictions of this day taught you?

October 31 ❀ Wondrous Things

Morning 86:8–10
Among the gods there is none like you, O Lord,
nor anything like your works.
All nations you have made will come and worship you, O Lord,
and glorify your Name.
For you are great;
you do wondrous things;
and you alone are God.

What helps you recognize wonders as works of God?

Evening 145:5–7
I will ponder the glorious splendor of your majesty
and all your marvelous works.

They shall speak of the might of your wondrous acts,
and I will tell of your greatness.
They shall publish the remembrance of your great goodness;
they shall sing of your righteous deeds.

How have you noticed God's goodness and wonders published today?

NOVEMBER

November 1 ❀ All Saints' Day

Morning 149:1–3
Hallelujah!
Sing to the LORD a new song;
sing his praise in the congregation of the faithful.
Let Israel rejoice in his Maker;
let the children of Zion be joyful in their King.
Let them praise his Name in the dance;
let them sing praise to him with timbrel and harp.

A hallmark of saints is their praise of God using their unique gifts.
Which of your gifts will *you* use to praise God today?

Evening 113:3–5
From the rising of the sun to its going down
let the Name of the Lord be praised.
The LORD is high above all nations,
and his glory above the heavens.
Who is like the LORD our God, who sits enthroned on high
but stoops to behold the heavens and the earth?

How does it shape your theology to think of God stooping?

November 2 ❀ All Souls' Day

Morning 130:1–3
Out of the depths have I called to you, O LORD;
LORD, hear my voice;
let your ears consider well the voice of my supplication.
If you, LORD, were to note what is done amiss,
O LORD, who could stand?
For there is forgiveness with you;
therefore you shall be feared.

Recognize that all souls come from the depths of God.

Evening 116:12–14
I will fulfill my vows to the LORD
in the presence of all his people.
Precious in the sight of the LORD
is the death of his servants.
O LORD, *I am your servant;*
I am your servant and the child of your handmaid;
you have freed me from my bonds.

Remember that *you* are also one of God's souls.

November 3 ❀ Vows

Morning 76:10–12
Truly, wrathful Edom will give you thanks,
and the remnant of Hamath will keep your feasts.
Make a vow to the LORD *your God and keep it;*
let all around him bring gifts to him who is worthy to be feared.
He breaks the spirit of princes,
and strikes terror in the kings of the earth.

What gifts do you intend to bring to God's world today?

Evening 78:34–37
Whenever he slew them, they would seek him,
and repent, and diligently search for God.
They would remember that God was their rock,
and the Most High God their redeemer.
But they flattered him with their mouths
and lied to him with their tongues.
Their heart was not steadfast toward him,
and they were not faithful to his covenant.

What makes you diligent in your search for God?

November 4 ❀ Unity with God

Morning 12:6
The words of the LORD *are pure words,*
like silver refined from ore
and purified seven times in the fire.

Seek to bring purity into your own words today.

Evening 10:15–16
The helpless commit themselves to you,
for you are the helper of orphans.
Break the power of the wicked and evil;
search out their wickedness until you find none.

Join with God by praying in the strength of love.

November 5 ❀ Humiliation

Morning 25:1–2
To you, O LORD, I lift up my soul;
my God, I put my trust in you;
let me not be humiliated,
nor let my enemies triumph over me.
Let none who look to you be put to shame;
let the treacherous be disappointed in their schemes.

Pray that you learn from times of humiliation.

Evening 109:15–16
Because he did not remember to show mercy,
but persecuted the poor and needy
and sought to kill the brokenhearted.
He loved cursing,
let it come upon him;
he took no delight in blessing,
let it depart from him.

One way deeds can be repaid is in how one casts votes for elected officials.

November 6 ❀ Renewal

Morning 119:164–165
Seven times a day do I praise you,
because of your righteous judgments.
Great peace have they who love your law;
for them there is no stumbling block.

Pause to praise God at least seven times today and notice its effects.

Evening 104:30–31
You hide your face, and they are terrified;

you take away their breath,
and they die and return to their dust.
You send forth your Spirit, and they are created;
and so you renew the face of the earth.

How have you seen God's renewal today?

November 7 ❈ Answer

Morning 20:1–4
May the LORD answer you in the day of trouble,
the Name of the God of Jacob defend you;
Send you help from his holy place
and strengthen you out of Zion;
Remember all your offerings
and accept your burnt sacrifice;
Grant you your heart's desire
and prosper all your plans.

Use these words as a prayer for someone in trouble.

Evening 103:19
The LORD has set his throne in heaven,
and his kingship has dominion over all.

Intentionally recognize that individuals, places, and events you love are all in God's dominion.

November 8 ❈ Sin's Presence

Morning 140:4–5
Keep me, O LORD, from the hands of the wicked;
protect me from the violent,
who are determined to trip me up.
The proud have hidden a snare for me
and stretched out a net of cords;
they have set traps for me along the path.

Pray for God's protection each time you see traps set for you today.

Evening 94:6–8
They murder the widow and the stranger
and put the orphans to death.
Yet they say, "The LORD does not see,

the God of Jacob takes no notice."
Consider well, you dullards among the people;
when will you fools understand?

What sins are you too "dull" to see?

November 9 ✤ Envy

Morning 129:5–8
Let them be put to shame and thrown back,
all those who are enemies of Zion.
Let them be like grass upon the housetops,
which withers before it can be plucked;
Which does not fill the hand of the reaper,
nor the bosom of him who binds the sheaves;
So that those who go by say not so much as,
"The LORD *prosper you.*
We wish you well in the Name of the LORD.*"*

Wish the ashamed well in the Name of the Lord.

Evening 68:16
Why do you look with envy, O rugged mountain,
at the hill which God chose for his resting place?
truly, the LORD *will dwell there for ever.*

What do you imagine God's dwelling is like?

November 10 ✤ Might

Morning 29:7
The voice of the LORD *splits the flames of fire;*
the voice of the LORD *shakes the wilderness;*
the LORD *shakes the wilderness of Kadesh.*

Do you tend to hear God's voice as powerful, resounding, or quiet?

Evening 110:5–7
The LORD *who is at your right hand*
will smite kings in the day of his wrath;
he will rule over the nations.
He will heap high the corpses;
he will smash heads over the wide earth.
He will drink from the brook beside the road;

therefore he will lift high his head.

What do you make of this image of God, who is distant and violent, while also humble enough to drink from a stream?

November 11 ✤ Strength

Morning 28:10–11
The LORD is the strength of his people,
a safe refuge for his anointed.
Save your people and bless your inheritance;
shepherd them and carry them for ever.

What does it mean to ask God to shepherd us?

Evening 89:41–45
All who pass by despoil him;
he has become the scorn of his neighbors.
You have exalted the right hand of his foes
and made all his enemies rejoice.
You have turned back the edge of his sword
and have not sustained him in battle.
You have put an end to his splendor
and cast his throne to the ground.
You have cut short the days of his youth
and have covered him with shame.

Who have you scorned today?

November 12 ✤ The Righteous

Morning 37:31–33
The righteous shall possess the land
and dwell in it for ever.
The mouth of the righteous utters wisdom,
and their tongue speaks what is right.
The law of their God is in their heart,
and their footsteps shall not falter.

Use your God-given wisdom to speak what is right today.

Evening 119:78–80
Let the arrogant be put to shame, for they wrong me with lies;
but I will meditate on your commandments.

Let those who fear you turn to me,
and also those who know your decrees.
Let my heart be sound in your statutes,
that I may not be put to shame.

Who among those who fear God turned toward you today?

November 13 ✿ Entering

Morning 118:19–20
Open for me the gates of righteousness;
I will enter them;
I will offer thanks to the LORD.
"This is the gate of the LORD;
he who is righteous may enter."

What gates will God open for you today?

Evening 132:7–9
Let us go to God's dwelling place;
let us fall upon our knees before his footstool."
Arise, O LORD, into your resting-place,
you and the ark of your strength.
Let your priests be clothed with righteousness;
let your faithful people sing with joy.

Rest with God this night.

November 14 ✿ Praise

Morning 47:6–8
Sing praises to God, sing praises;
sing praises to our King, sing praises.
For God is King of all the earth;
sing praises with all your skill.
God reigns over the nations;
God sits upon his holy throne.

How will you praise God today?

Evening 137:1–4
By the waters of Babylon we sat down and wept,
when we remembered you, O Zion.
As for our harps, we hung them up

on the trees in the midst of that land.
For those who led us away captive asked us for a song,
and our oppressors called for mirth:
"Sing us one of the songs of Zion."
How shall we sing the LORD's song
upon an alien soil?

If you have you felt yourself on alien soil today, what did you do to mitigate the sense of being a stranger?

November 15 ❀ Deliverance

Morning 96:1–3
Sing to the LORD a new song;
sing to the LORD, all the whole earth.
Sing to the LORD and bless his Name;
proclaim the good news of his salvation from day to day.
Declare his glory among the nations
and his wonders among all peoples.

Let your life proclaim God's glory!

Evening 17:10–13
They have closed their heart to pity,
and their mouth speaks proud things.
They press me hard,
now they surround me,
watching how they may cast me to the ground,
Like a lion, greedy for its prey,
and like a young lion lurking in secret places.
Arise, O LORD; confront them and bring them down;
deliver me from the wicked by your sword.

However you envisage the wicked in your life, you may offer them to God this night.

November 16 ❀ Fading

Morning 37:1–3
Do not fret yourself because of evildoers;
do not be jealous of those who do wrong.
For they shall soon wither like the grass,
and like the green grass fade away.

Put your trust in the LORD and do good;
dwell in the land and feed on its riches.

Imagine the power of evildoers in your life fading away.

Evening 79:4–7
We have become a reproach to our neighbors,
an object of scorn and derision to those around us.
How long will you be angry, O LORD?
will your fury blaze like fire for ever?
Pour out your wrath upon the heathen who have not known you
and upon the kingdoms that have not called upon your Name.
For they have devoured Jacob
and made his dwelling a ruin.

Do you assume that your anger is aligned with God's anger?

November 17 ❀ Sovereignty

Morning 83:16–18
Cover their faces with shame, O LORD,
that they may seek your Name.
Let them be disgraced and terrified for ever;
let them be put to confusion and perish.
Let them know that you, whose Name is YAHWEH,
you alone are the Most High over all the earth.

Be a cheerleader for God today!

Evening 48:4–6
Behold, the kings of the earth assembled
and marched forward together.
They looked and were astounded;
they retreated and fled in terror.
Trembling seized them there;
they writhed like a woman in childbirth,
like ships of the sea when the east wind shatters them.

How would you describe yourself in fear?

November 18 ❀ Accusation

Morning 95:8–9
Harden not your hearts,

as your forebears did in the wilderness,
at Meribah, and on that day at Massah,
when they tempted me.
They put me to the test,
though they had seen my works.

Seek to soften your heart.

Evening 50:22–24
"I have made my accusation;
I have put my case in order before your eyes.
Consider this well, you who forget God,
lest I rend you and there be none to deliver you.
Whoever offers me the sacrifice of thanksgiving honors me;
but to those who keep in my way will I show the salvation of God."

How have you made a case for God today?

November 19 ❀ Persecution

Morning 78:9–11
The people of Ephraim, armed with the bow,
turned back in the day of battle;
They did not keep the covenant of God,
and refused to walk in his law;
They forgot what he had done,
and the wonders he had shown them.

Pledge to remember your faith throughout the day.

Evening 119:85–88
The proud have dug pits for me;
they do not keep your law.
All your commandments are true;
help me, for they persecute me with lies.
They had almost made an end of me on earth,
but I have not forsaken your commandments.
In your loving-kindness, revive me,
that I may keep the decrees of your mouth.

Have you felt persecuted today?

November 20 ❀ Continuity

Morning 102:28
The children of your servants shall continue,
and their offspring shall stand fast in your sight."

Pray especially for children today.

Evening 74:11–14
Yet God is my King from ancient times,
victorious in the midst of the earth.
You divided the sea by your might
and shattered the heads of the dragons upon the waters;
You crushed the heads of Leviathan
and gave him to the people of the desert for food.
You split open spring and torrent;
you dried up ever-flowing rivers.

What do you find most impressive about God's creativity?

November 21 ❀ Remembering

Morning 128:5–6
The LORD bless you from Zion,
and may you see the prosperity of Jerusalem all the days of your life.
May you live to see your children's children;
may peace be upon Israel.

Remember to pray for God's blessing on others today.

Evening 31:12–14
I am forgotten like a dead man, out of mind;
I am as useless as a broken pot.
For I have heard the whispering of the crowd;
fear is all around;
they put their heads together against me;
they plot to take my life.
But as for me, I have trusted in you, O LORD.
I have said, "You are my God.

There is always security in God.

November 22 ❧ Threat

Morning 22:12–13
Many young bulls encircle me;
strong bulls of Bashan surround me.
They open wide their jaws at me,
like a ravening and a roaring lion.

What threatens you?

Evening 126:1–4
When the LORD *restored the fortunes of Zion,*
then were we like those who dream.
Then was our mouth filled with laughter,
and our tongue with shouts of joy.
Then they said among the nations,
"The LORD *has done great things for them."*
The LORD *has done great things for us,*
and we are glad indeed.

Fortunes can be restored; laughter can replace shouts of distress.

November 23 ❧ God's Devices

Morning 81:10–13
I am the LORD *your God,*
who brought you out of the land of Egypt and said,
"Open your mouth wide, and I will fill it."
And yet my people did not hear my voice,
and Israel would not obey me.
So I gave them over to the stubbornness of their hearts,
to follow their own devices.
Oh, that my people would listen to me!
that Israel would walk in my ways!

Live today seeking to follow God's devices.

Evening 68:14–15
When the Almighty scattered kings,
it was like snow falling in Zalmon.
O mighty mountain, O hill of Bashan!
O rugged mountain, O hill of Bashan!

How have you noticed God's acts in nature?

November 24 ❀ Tests

Morning 119:94–95
I am yours; oh, that you would save me!
for I study your commandments.
Though the wicked lie in wait for me to destroy me,
I will apply my mind to your decrees.

Focus on God as a defense against the wicked.

Evening 7:8–10
Be seated on your lofty throne, O Most High;
O LORD, judge the nations.
Give judgment for me according to my righteousness, O LORD,
and according to my innocence, O Most High.
Let the malice of the wicked come to an end,
but establish the righteous;
for you test the mind and heart, O righteous God.

Have you felt tested by God today?

November 25 ❀ Integrity

Morning 25:19–20
Protect my life and deliver me;
let me not be put to shame, for I have trusted in you.
Let integrity and uprightness preserve me,
for my hope has been in you.

Wear integrity as a shield today.

Evening 94:20–23
Can a corrupt tribunal have any part with you,
one which frames evil into law?
They conspire against the life of the just
and condemn the innocent to death.
But the LORD has become my stronghold,
and my God the rock of my trust.
He will turn their wickedness back upon them
and destroy them in their own malice;
the LORD our God will destroy them.

God offers you security against evil.

November 26 ❀ Sacrifices

Morning 66:12–13

I will enter your house with burnt-offerings
and will pay you my vows,
which I promised with my lips
and spoke with my mouth when I was in trouble.
I will offer you sacrifices of fat beasts
with the smoke of rams;
I will give you oxen and goats.

What kinds of vows and sacrifices can you offer God today?

Evening 103:12–14

As far as the east is from the west,
so far has he removed our sins from us.
As a father cares for his children,
so does the LORD care for those who fear him.
For he himself knows whereof we are made;
he remembers that we are but dust.

How would these words speak to you if "father" were modified with the word "good"?

November 27 ❀ Thanksgiving

Morning 50:13–15

"Do you think I eat the flesh of bulls,
or drink the blood of goats?
Offer to God a sacrifice of thanksgiving
and make good your vows to the Most High.
Call upon me in the day of trouble;
I will deliver you, and you shall honor me."

Consider that calling upon God in trouble is what God desires.

Evening 31:3

Be my strong rock, a castle to keep me safe,
for you are my crag and my stronghold;
for the sake of your Name, lead me and guide me.

What is there about God's castle that keeps you safe?

November 28 ❖ Power

Morning 116:15–17
I will offer you the sacrifice of thanksgiving
and call upon the Name of the LORD.
I will fulfill my vows to the LORD
in the presence of all his people,
In the courts of the LORD's house,
in the midst of you, O Jerusalem.
Hallelujah!

What does "sacrifice of thanksgiving" mean to you?

Evening 18:41–43
I destroy those who hate me;
they cry out, but there is none to help them;
they cry to the LORD, but he does not answer.
I beat them small like dust before the wind;
I trample them like mud in the streets.
You deliver me from the strife of the peoples;
you put me at the head of the nations.

How legitimate is the power that you experience?

November 29 ❖ Faith

Morning 20:7–9
Some put their trust in chariots and some in horses,
but we will call upon the Name of the LORD our God.
They collapse and fall down,
but we will arise and stand upright.
O LORD, give victory to the king
and answer us when we call.

Who aids you in calling on God?

Evening 119:139–141
My indignation has consumed me,
because my enemies forget your words.
Your word has been tested to the uttermost,
and your servant holds it dear.
I am small and of little account,

yet I do not forget your commandments.

What makes you indignant?

November 30 ❀ Failing Spirit

Morning 143:7–8

O LORD, make haste to answer me; my spirit fails me;
do not hide your face from me
or I shall be like those who go down to the Pit.
Let me hear of your loving-kindness in the morning,
for I put my trust in you;
show me the road that I must walk,
for I lift up my soul to you.

What road do you think God is inviting you to walk?

Evening 4:6–8

Many are saying,
"Oh, that we might see better times!"
Lift up the light of your countenance upon us, O LORD.
You have put gladness in my heart,
more than when grain and wine and oil increase.
I lie down in peace; at once I fall asleep;
for only you, LORD, make me dwell in safety.

Meditate on that which makes you glad as you fall asleep.

DECEMBER

December 1 ❀ Everlasting

Morning 10:12–14
Rise up, O LORD;
lift up your hand, O God;
do not forget the afflicted.
Why should the wicked revile God?
why should they say in their heart, "You do not care"?
Surely, you behold trouble and misery;
you see it and take it into your own hand.
Offer to God any trouble and misery you see today.

Evening 119:89–91
O LORD, your word is everlasting;
it stands firm in the heavens.
Your faithfulness remains from one generation to another;
you established the earth, and it abides.
By your decree these continue to this day,
for all things are your servants.
Recall the best example of a faithful servant you witnessed today.

December 2 ❀ Promise

Morning 12:5
"Because the needy are oppressed,
and the poor cry out in misery,
I will rise up," says the LORD,
"and give them the help they long for."
What help do you long for?

Evening 37:11–12
In a little while the wicked shall be no more;
you shall search out their place, but they will not be there.
But the lowly shall possess the land;

they will delight in abundance of peace.

How have you experienced abundance of peace?

December 3 ❈ God's Omnipresence

Morning 94:9–10
He that planted the ear, does he not hear?
he that formed the eye, does he not see?
He who admonishes the nations, will he not punish?
he who teaches all the world, has he no knowledge?

What do you think angers God most?

Evening 77:17–18
The clouds poured out water;
the skies thundered;
your arrows flashed to and fro;
The sound of your thunder was in the whirlwind;
your lightnings lit up the world;
the earth trembled and shook.

What do you think the world's reaction will be to the celebration of Christ's birth?

December 4 ❈ Discouraged

Morning 145:14
The LORD is faithful in all his words
and merciful in all his deeds.

Repeat this verse to yourself today when you feel discouraged.

Evening 129:1–4
"Greatly have they oppressed me since my youth,"
let Israel now say;
"Greatly have they oppressed me since my youth,
but they have not prevailed against me."
The plowmen plowed upon my back
and made their furrows long.
The LORD, the Righteous One,
has cut the cords of the wicked.

Have you been able to find hope today?

December 5 ❈ Mercy

Morning 65:1–3
You are to be praised, O God, in Zion;
to you shall vows be performed in Jerusalem.
To you that hear prayer shall all flesh come,
because of their transgressions.
Our sins are stronger than we are,
but you will blot them out.

Much like Lent, Advent is traditionally a time of repentance. What past actions do you want God to blot out?

Evening 119:129–132
Your decrees are wonderful;
therefore I obey them with all my heart.
When your word goes forth it gives light;
it gives understanding to the simple.
I open my mouth and pant;
I long for your commandments.
Turn to me in mercy,
as you always do to those who love your Name.

How have you experienced God's light in God's word?

December 6 ❈ Power

Morning 74:20–22
Let not the oppressed turn away ashamed;
let the poor and needy praise your Name.
Arise, O God, maintain your cause;
remember how fools revile you all day long.
Forget not the clamor of your adversaries,
the unending tumult of those who rise up against you.

How can you help maintain God's cause today?

Evening 109:26–27
Let them know that this is your hand,
that you, O LORD, have done it.
They may curse, but you will bless;
let those who rise up against me be put to shame,

and your servant will rejoice.
Recall times you have witnessed God's power.

December 7 ❀ Deliverance

Morning 141:4–7
Let me not be occupied in wickedness with evildoers,
nor eat of their choice foods.
Let the righteous smite me in friendly rebuke;
let not the oil of the unrighteous anoint my head;
for my prayer is continually against their wicked deeds.
Let their rulers be overthrown in stony places,
that they may know my words are true.
As when a plowman turns over the earth in furrows,
let their bones be scattered at the mouth of the grave.

Avoid evildoers as you would avoid poisoned food.

Evening 31:1–2
In you, O LORD, have I taken refuge;
let me never be put to shame;
deliver me in your righteousness.
Incline your ear to me;
make haste to deliver me.

Pray about the meaning of being delivered.

December 8 ❀ Crushed Spirit

Morning 34:15–19
The eyes of the LORD are upon the righteous,
and his ears are open to their cry.
The face of the LORD is against those who do evil,
to root out the remembrance of them from the earth.
The righteous cry, and the LORD hears them
and delivers them from all their troubles.
The LORD is near to the brokenhearted
and will save those whose spirits are crushed.
Many are the troubles of the righteous,
but the LORD will deliver him out of them all.

How do you imagine the face of God?

Evening 90:13

Return, O LORD; how long will you tarry?
be gracious to your servants.

Meditate on God's graciousness.

December 9 ❀ Remember

Morning 63:1–2

O God, you are my God; eagerly I seek you;
my soul thirsts for you, my flesh faints for you,
as in a barren and dry land where there is no water.
Therefore I have gazed upon you in your holy place,
that I might behold your power and your glory.

Advent is about seeking God.

Evening 132:1–5

LORD, remember David,
and all the hardships he endured;
How he swore an oath to the LORD
and vowed a vow to the Mighty One of Jacob:
"I will not come under the roof of my house,"
nor climb up into my bed;
I will not allow my eyes to sleep,
nor let my eyelids slumber;
Until I find a place for the LORD,
a dwelling for the Mighty One of Jacob."

How do you vow to find a dwelling for Jesus?

December 10 ❀ Rejection

Morning 73:4–6

For they suffer no pain,
and their bodies are sleek and sound;
In the misfortunes of others they have no share;
they are not afflicted as others are;
Therefore they wear their pride like a necklace
and wrap their violence about them like a cloak.

What do you wear as a necklace?

Evening 118:21–24

I will give thanks to you, for you answered me
and have become my salvation.
The same stone which the builders rejected
has become the chief cornerstone.
This is the LORD's doing,
and it is marvelous in our eyes.
On this day the LORD has acted;
we will rejoice and be glad in it.

What of the Lord's doing is marvelous in your eyes?

December 11 ❀ Justice

Morning 140:11–13

A slanderer shall not be established on the earth,
and evil shall hunt down the lawless.
I know that the LORD will maintain the cause of the poor
and render justice to the needy.
Surely, the righteous will give thanks to your Name,
and the upright shall continue in your sight.

Recognition of God's care for the needy and the oppressed is a major theme of Advent.

Evening 84:3–4

Happy are they who dwell in your house!
they will always be praising you.
Happy are the people whose strength is in you!
whose hearts are set on the pilgrims' way.

In what ways are you a pilgrim?

December 12 ❀ Awe

Morning 22:22–24

Praise the LORD, you that fear him;
stand in awe of him, O offspring of Israel;
all you of Jacob's line, give glory.
For he does not despise nor abhor the poor in their poverty;
neither does he hide his face from them;
but when they cry to him he hears them.

My praise is of him in the great assembly;
I will perform my vows in the presence of those who worship him.

Do not abhor the poor.

Evening 91:8–10
Your eyes have only to behold
to see the reward of the wicked.
Because you have made the LORD your refuge,
and the Most High your habitation,
There shall no evil happen to you,
neither shall any plague come near your dwelling.

Make the Most High your habitation as you sleep.

December 13 ✤ Rescue

Morning 72:1–4
Give the King your justice, O God,
and your righteousness to the King's Son;
That he may rule your people righteously
and the poor with justice;
That the mountains may bring prosperity to the people,
and the little hills bring righteousness.
He shall defend the needy among the people;
he shall rescue the poor and crush the oppressor.

Pray that God will inspire the powerful to rule with justice for the sake of the poor.

Evening 111:7–8
The works of his hands are faithfulness and justice;
all his commandments are sure.
They stand fast for ever and ever,
because they are done in truth and equity.

Look forward to the birth of Christ.

December 14 ✤ Keeping Promises

Morning 146:4–7
Happy are they who have the God of Jacob for their help!
whose hope is in the LORD their God;
Who made heaven and earth, the seas, and all that is in them;

who keeps his promise for ever;
Who gives justice to those who are oppressed,
and food to those who hunger.
The LORD sets the prisoners free;
the LORD opens the eyes of the blind;
the LORD lifts up those who are bowed down.

How, and to what, has God opened your eyes?

Evening 134 (entire psalm)
Behold now, bless the LORD, all you servants of the LORD,
you that stand by night in the house of the LORD.
Lift up your hands in the holy place and bless the LORD;
the LORD who made heaven and earth bless you out of Zion.

For what do you bless God tonight?

December 15 ❃ Everlasting

Morning 119:96
I see that all things come to an end,
but your commandment has no bounds.

Watch for God's boundless-ness today.

Evening 135:13–14
O LORD, your Name is everlasting;
your renown, O LORD, endures from age to age.
For the LORD gives his people justice
and shows compassion to his servants.

Have you helped the Lord give people justice today?

December 16 ❃ Liberation

Morning 145:15–18
The LORD upholds all those who fall;
he lifts up those who are bowed down.
The eyes of all wait upon you, O LORD,
and you give them their food in due season.
You open wide your hand
and satisfy the needs of every living creature.
The LORD is righteous in all his ways

and loving in all his works.

Advent is a season of waiting for God's promise of liberation. Pray for that from which you desire liberation.

Evening 10:9–11
They lie in wait, like a lion in a covert;
they lie in wait to seize upon the lowly;
they seize the lowly and drag them away in their net.
The innocent are broken and humbled before them;
the helpless fall before their power.
They say in their heart, "God has forgotten;
he hides his face; he will never notice."

Meditate on the cowardliness of oppressors.

December 17 ❀ Judgment

Morning 69:34–36
The afflicted shall see and be glad;
you who seek God, your heart shall live.
For the LORD listens to the needy,
and his prisoners he does not despise.
Let the heavens and the earth praise him,
the seas and all that moves in them.

Let your heart live today.

Evening 50:3–6
Our God will come and will not keep silence;
before him there is a consuming flame,
and round about him a raging storm.
He calls the heavens and the earth from above
to witness the judgment of his people.
"Gather before me my loyal followers,
those who have made a covenant with me
and sealed it with sacrifice."
Let the heavens declare the rightness of his cause;
for God himself is judge.

How do you feel about God as a judge?

December 18 ❀ Defense

Morning 82:3–5
Save the weak and the orphan;
defend the humble and needy;
Rescue the weak and the poor;
deliver them from the power of the wicked.
They do not know, neither do they understand;
they go about in darkness;
all the foundations of the earth are shaken.

Walk in the light.

Evening 72:15–16
Long may he live!
and may there be given to him gold from Arabia;
may prayer be made for him always,
and may they bless him all the day long.
May there be abundance of grain on the earth,
growing thick even on the hilltops;
may its fruit flourish like Lebanon,
and its grain like grass upon the earth.

How do you understand the relationship between worship and abundance?

December 19 ❀ Compassion

Morning 102:13–14
You will arise and have compassion on Zion,
for it is time to have mercy upon her;
indeed, the appointed time has come.
For your servants love her very rubble,
and are moved to pity even for her dust.

What moves you to pity on God's behalf?

Evening 88:15–16
Lord, why have you rejected me?
why have you hidden your face from me?
Ever since my youth, I have been wretched and at the point of death;
I have borne your terrors with a troubled mind.

God is the best place for a troubled mind.

December 20 ❀ Lions

Morning 91:11–13
For he shall give his angels charge over you,
to keep you in all your ways.
They shall bear you in their hands,
lest you dash your foot against a stone.
You shall tread upon the lion and adder;
you shall trample the young lion and the serpent under your feet.

Face today aware of your strength in God.

Evening 35:17–19
*O L*ORD*, how long will you look on?*
rescue me from the roaring beasts,
and my life from the young lions.
I will give you thanks in the great congregation;
I will praise you in the mighty throng.
Do not let my treacherous foes rejoice over me,
nor let those who hate me without a cause wink at each other.

Impatience can be transformed into calm certainty by God.

December 21 ❀ Patience

Morning 37:4–7
*Take delight in the L*ORD*,*
and he shall give you your heart's desire.
*Commit your way to the L*ORD *and put your trust in him,*
and he will bring it to pass.
He will make your righteousness as clear as the light
and your just dealing as the noonday.
*Be still before the L*ORD
and wait patiently for him.

Delight in patience as you wait for Christ's birth.

Evening 40:17–19
Let all who seek you rejoice in you and be glad;
let those who love your salvation continually say,
*"Great is the L*ORD*!"*
Though I am poor and afflicted,
*the L*ORD *will have regard for me.*

You are my helper and my deliverer;
do not tarry, O my God.

Pray for all those who are poor and afflicted that God will soon fill
their needs, and that you can be a helper.

December 22 ❀ Victory

Morning 20:5–6
We will shout for joy at your victory
and triumph in the Name of our God;
may the LORD grant all your requests.
Now I know that the LORD gives victory to his anointed;
he will answer him out of his holy heaven,
with the victorious strength of his right hand.

Look for God's victorious strength today.

Evening 145:19–20
The LORD is near to those who call upon him,
to all who call upon him faithfully.
He fulfills the desire of those who fear him;
he hears their cry and helps them.

Have you felt your cries heard today?

December 23 ❀ Doors

Morning 24:7
Lift up your heads, O gates;
lift them high, O everlasting doors;
and the King of glory shall come in.

Are you prepared for Christ's entrance into your life?

Evening 9:9–11
The LORD will be a refuge for the oppressed,
a refuge in time of trouble.
Those who know your Name will put their trust in you,
for you never forsake those who seek you, O LORD.
Sing praise to the Lord who dwells in Zion;
proclaim to the peoples the things he has done.

Praise God with your trust.

December 24 ❀ Fruit

Morning 27:17–18
What if I had not believed
that I should see the goodness of the LORD
in the land of the living!
O tarry and await the LORD's pleasure;
be strong, and he shall comfort your heart;
wait patiently for the Lord.

Advent, and the waiting it requires for Christ's birth, offers a gift of strength.

Evening 132:11–13
The LORD has sworn an oath to David;
in truth, he will not break it:
"A son, the fruit of your body
will I set upon your throne.
If your children keep my covenant
and my testimonies that I shall teach them,
their children will sit upon your throne for evermore."

How can you pass along the miracle of Christ's birth to children?

December 25 ❀ Christmas Day

Morning 96:11–13
Let the heavens rejoice, and let the earth be glad;
let the sea thunder and all that is in it;
let the field be joyful and all that is therein.
Then shall all the trees of the wood shout for joy
before the LORD when he comes,
when he comes to judge the earth.
He will judge the world with righteousness
and the peoples with his truth.

Accept God's invitation to rejoice at Christ's birth.

Evening 97:10–12
The LORD loves those who hate evil;
he preserves the lives of his saints
and delivers them from the hand of the wicked.
Light has sprung up for the righteous,

and joyful gladness for those who are truehearted.
Rejoice in the LORD, you righteous,
and give thanks to his holy Name.

For what are you most thankful this Christmas night?

December 26 ❀ Joy

Morning 81:1–3
Sing with joy to God our strength
and raise a loud shout to the God of Jacob.
Raise a song and sound the timbrel,
the merry harp, and the lyre.
Blow the ram's-horn at the new moon,
and at the full moon, the day of our feast.

This is the feasting season of Christmas. How do you intend to contribute to the feast?

Evening 112:7–9
They will not be afraid of any evil rumors;
their heart is right;
they put their trust in the LORD.
Their heart is established and will not shrink,
until they see their desire upon their enemies.
They have given freely to the poor,
and their righteousness stands fast for ever;
they will hold up their head with honor.

How does it make you feel to be a giver?

December 27 ❀ Exaltation

Morning 57:6–11
Exalt yourself above the heavens, O God,
and your glory over all the earth.
My heart is firmly fixed, O God, my heart is fixed;
I will sing and make melody.
Wake up, my spirit;
awake, lute and harp;
I myself will waken the dawn.
I will confess you among the peoples, O LORD;
I will sing praise to you among the nations.

For your loving-kindness is greater than the heavens,
and your faithfulness reaches to the clouds.
Exalt yourself above the heavens, O God,
and your glory over all the earth.

Waken the dawn exalting in God!

Evening 96:10
Tell it out among the nations: "The LORD is King!
he has made the world so firm that it cannot be moved;
he will judge the peoples with equity."

What have you told the world today?

December 28 ❀ Rule

Morning 82:8
Arise, O God, and rule the earth,
for you shall take all nations for your own.

Imagine a world in which all nations are aware of belonging to God.

Evening 68:11–13
The LORD gave the word;
great was the company of women who bore the tidings:
"Kings with their armies are fleeing away;
the women at home are dividing the spoils."
Though you lingered among the sheepfolds,
you shall be like a dove whose wings are covered with silver,
whose feathers are like green gold."

Christmas tidings are yours.

December 29 ❀ God's Power

Morning 68:17–18
The chariots of God are twenty thousand,
even thousands of thousands;
the LORD comes in holiness from Sinai.
You have gone up on high and led captivity captive;
you have received gifts even from your enemies,
that the LORD God might dwell among them.

What do you think God desires to be held captive?

Evening 36:5–9
Your love, O LORD, reaches to the heavens,
and your faithfulness to the clouds.
Your righteousness is like the strong mountains,
your justice like the great deep;
you save both man and beast, O LORD.
How priceless is your love, O God!
your people take refuge under the shadow of your wings.
They feast upon the abundance of your house;
you give them drink from the river of your delights.
For with you is the well of life,
and in your light we see light.

How are you experiencing God's abundance of light in Christmas, this
season of delight?

December 30 ❋ Thanks

Morning 147:17–21
He gives snow like wool;
he scatters hoarfrost like ashes.
He scatters his hail like bread crumbs;
who can stand against his cold?
He sends forth his word and melts them;
he blows with his wind, and the waters flow.
He declares his word to Jacob,
his statutes and his judgments to Israel.
He has not done so to any other nation;
to them he has not revealed his judgments.
Hallelujah!

Notice God in the winter.

Evening 56:10–12
In God the LORD, whose word I praise,
in God I trust and will not be afraid,
for what can mortals do to me?
I am bound by the vow I made to you, O God;
I will present to you thank-offerings;
For you have rescued my soul from death and my feet from stumbling,
that I may walk before God in the light of the living.

Offer God thanks!

December 31 ❀ Praise

Morning 150:3–6

Praise him with the blast of the ram's-horn;
praise him with lyre and harp.
Praise him with timbrel and dance;
praise him with strings and pipe.
Praise him with resounding cymbals;
praise him with loud-clanging cymbals.
Let everything that has breath
praise the LORD.
Hallelujah!

Notice the ways in which everything that has breath praises the Lord.

Evening 23:5–6

You spread a table before me in the presence of those who trouble me;
you have anointed my head with oil,
and my cup is running over.
Surely your goodness and mercy shall follow me all the days of my life,
and I will dwell in the house of the LORD for ever.

Go to sleep knowing that goodness and mercy shall follow you into the new year.

RECOMMENDED
RESOURCES

The Book of Common Prayer: According to the Use of the Episcopal Church. New York: Church Publishing, 1979.

Bourgeault, Cynthia. *Singing the Psalms.* Boulder, CO: Sounds True, 1997.

Brueggemann, Walter. *The Psalms and the Life of Faith.* Minneapolis: Fortress Press, 1995.

Cross, F. L. and E. A. Livingstone. *The Oxford Dictionary of the Christian Church.* New York: Oxford University Press, 1990.

Fisch, Harold. *Poetry with a Purpose: Biblical Poetics and Interpretation.* Bloomington, IN: Indiana University Press, 1988.

Meeks, Wayne A., general editor, Jouette M. Bassler, Werner E. Lemke, Susan Niditch, and Eileen M. Schuller, associate editors. *The Harper Collins Study Bible: New Revised Standard Version.* New York: Harper-Collins Publishers, 1993.

Miller, David L. "Psalms and Sighs." *The Lutheran* (December 1997): 13–14.

Shannon, Martin. "The Psalter: A School of Prayer." *Crosspoint* (Spring 2001): 24–30.

Westermann, Claus. *The Psalms: Structure, Content and Message.* Minneapolis: Augsburg Publishing House, 1980.

Meditations on the Psalms
for Every Day of the Year
Barbara Cawthorne Crafton

The Psalms, written centuries ago, are filled with the same emotions and issues that challenge, comfort, and confound us today. Their complaints, joys, celebrations, fears, and hopes are ours as well. In this book of meditations for each day of the year, best-selling author Barbara Crafton combines reflection on these ancient texts with contemporary stories to help us explore the spiritual nature of our lives. With gentle humor and unfailing honesty, she uses the Psalms to explore our deepest concerns: our faith, our spirits, and our relationship with God.

From starting anew in January to remembering to lighten up in December, Crafton's tough, warm-hearted, and beautifully written meditations are the perfect daily companion for anyone who finds nourishment in biblically based devotional reading.

Barbara Cawthorne Crafton is an Episcopal priest and a popular preacher, retreat leader, and writer. Her articles and reviews have appeared in the *New York Times*, *Reader's Digest*, *Family Circle*, *Glamour*, and *Episcopal Life*, among others. She is the author of many books, including *Let Every Heart Prepare*, *Living Lent*, *The Sewing Room*, and *Some Things You Just Have to Live With*, all available from Morehouse Publishing.

Morehouse books on spirituality are available through bookstores, on the Web, or directly from the publisher.

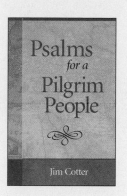

Psalms for a Pilgrim People

Jim Cotter

While the Psalms, written in ages long past, still speak to today's reader, there are many passages that are troubling. *Psalms for a Pilgrim People*, neither a translation nor a paraphrase, retains the poetry and beauty of the originals while making them come alive for the 21st-century reader. Readers will find this an inspiring book that takes today's realities into account by including references to present-day issues of concern.

Jim Cotter, a priest in the Church of England, focuses his ministry on writing books of prayers and reflection, seeking to unfold the Christian inheritance in fresh ways. A popular retreat leader, he visits the United States frequently.

"Cotter has broken open the psalms and made them speak of the Christian experience of God and of our century, of great progress, conflict, horror, and insecurity. These are psalms a First World Christian moving into the Third Millennium can pray without reservation or hesitation." —Christopher L. Webber, author, *The New Metrical Psalter* and *Praise the Lord, My Soul: Psalm 104 for Children*

"With new turns of phrase Cotter opens to his readers new insights into the Psalms' rich and enduring spirituality." —*Bible Collectors' World*

Morehouse books on spirituality are available through bookstores, on the Web, or directly from the publisher.